Child, Victim, Soldier

Sunday Obote

CHILD,
VICTIM,
SOLDIER

The Loss of Innocence in Uganda

DONALD H. DUNSON

ORBIS BOOKS

Maryknoll, New York 10545

Founded in 1970, Orbis Books endeavors to publish works that enlighten the mind, nourish the spirit, and challenge the conscience. The publishing arm of the Maryknoll Fathers and Brothers, Orbis seeks to explore the global dimensions of the Christian faith and mission, to invite dialogue with diverse cultures and religious traditions, and to serve the cause of reconciliation and peace. The books published reflect the views of their authors and do not represent the official position of the Maryknoll Society. To learn more about Maryknoll and Orbis Books, please visit our website at www.maryknoll.org.

Library of Congress Cataloging-in-Publication Data

Dunson, Donald H.
    Child, victim, soldier : the loss of innocence in Uganda / Donald H. Dunson.
        p. cm.
    ISBN-13: 978-1-57075-799-0 (pbk.)
    1. Children and war—Uganda. 2. Child soldiers—Uganda. 3. Children and violence—Uganda. 4. Political violence—Uganda. 5. Psychic trauma in children—Uganda. 6. Children—Uganda—Social conditions. 7. Lord's Resistance Army. 8. Kony, Joseph. I. Title.
    HQ784.W3D85 2008
    261.8'328096761—dc22

                                                              2008016458

Contents

Acknowledgments

God's gracious providence has brought me to the people and the experiences you will encounter in this book. The very first child soldier whom I met was Sunday Obote. He opened a door for me that has become a floodgate, and I will be eternally grateful that God has gifted me with Sunday's presence. His witness and amazing resilience have drawn me deeply into the plight of these children, some now young adults, struggling to reclaim their lives from their rebel captors. I happily dedicate all the efforts of this project to Sunday.

I am particularly indebted to three persons who walked with me in a special way during the process of writing this book, giving much greater depth and clarity to the work.

Lyn Travis, a Cuyahoga County assistant prosecutor in Ohio, accompanied me to the war zone of northern Uganda in 2007. She undertook extensive interviews of numerous formerly abducted child soldiers using her expertise of interviewing victims of crime in Cleveland. Her assistance added invaluable source material.

Gerard Thomas Straub, a documentary filmmaker, came to Uganda several times in 2007. We collaborated in chronicling the plight of the child soldiers in Gulu. He has the gift of capturing on film humanity's crushing moments and bringing them to the world. Through his documentary *The Fragrant Spirit of Life*, he draws us into the plight of the child soldiers whose stories you read in these pages. His creative enterprises compel all of us to find ways to be in solidarity with them.

Laura McBride has served as my graduate assistant during the writing of *Child, Victim, Soldier*. Her energy and passion for the children have moved this project forward in a way I could never have done by myself.

Numerous colleagues and friends read preliminary drafts and offered judicious insights that contributed substantively to the final text. Father Thomas Schubeck, who convenes an Ethics Writers Group at John Carroll University, and his colleagues in the group offered invaluable suggestions at the beginning of this project. Father Paul Hritz, Father Gerald Bednar, Father Paul Donahue, Ursuline Sister Mary McCormick, my nephew James A. Dunson III, Dr. Ted Raddell, Dr. Paula Ogrocki, Michael Regan, Denise Feyes, and the Sisters at the Carmel of the Holy Family in Cleveland Heights all generously gave of their time and talent in this endeavor. Alan Rome, librarian at St. Mary Seminary, provided invaluable research assistance throughout the project. And I am ever grateful to Father Thomas W. Tifft, rector at St. Mary Seminary, for his personal encouragement throughout my research and ministry.

Once again, God has mightily blessed me with the expertise of Susan Perry at Orbis Books as my editor. Her talent and care shine through every page.

Foreword

Our planet and its people are in a time of escalating peril. Environmental destruction has been escalating ever since the advent of the Industrial Revolution. Only now are we becoming ever more vigilant in our care for Mother Earth, respecting the integrity and innate goodness of the world we are blessed to inhabit. In our day, genocides of massive proportions have been unleashed in many regions of our world in ways harming all humanity. In my tiny corner of the planet in East Africa, these past three decades have witnessed several separate genocides inflicted on our sisters and brothers. In two nations that border my own, Sudan and Rwanda, recent violent conflicts have caught the attention of the entire global community. At the same time, in my own archdiocese in northern Uganda, among the people I love, there has been slow, massive death and destruction of the Acholi people unfolding throughout the past two decades. For many years this massive death and violence have gone relatively unnoticed by those living beyond the borders of Africa. I thank God for Father Donald Dunson who, among others, has come to live with us and to now tell our story to all who live at a great distance from us but who wish to be united with our struggles.

Brother Jesus taught us that we are the keepers of our brothers and sisters, wherever they live. We are one human family, whatever our national, racial, ethnic, economic, or ideological differences. The virtue of solidarity means precisely acknowledging that loving our neighbor has global dimensions in an ever increasingly interdependent world. This crucial insight I see enfleshed everywhere in the compelling writings of Donald Dunson, a friend of mine and, more important, a proven friend of the children in northern Uganda who have suffered too much at the hands of evil men.

As a moral theologian, Father Dunson has made a singular contribution to the efforts now being made to chronicle the events that unfolded in Acholiland these past two decades. In *Child, Victim, Sol-*

dier, he offers a moral and ethical reflection on the consequences of the war staged by the Lord's Resistance Army, in particular the spiritual consequences borne by its youngest and most vulnerable victims.

Who bears personal responsibility for this tragic sequence of events that has haunted the young lives of the children I serve in the Gulu Archdiocese? The answer is not as easy or as straightforward as many believe. I myself have felt guilty for not securing a more peaceful environment in my country for our young people to inherit. I have knelt before the children repeatedly and in shame, begging their forgiveness. The gift of this book lies in its ability to show forth the visible and invisible ties and responsibilities we all bear for one another and for the creation of a more humane and peaceful world.

In April 1997, three years after the genocide in Rwanda, the Symposium of Episcopal Conferences of Africa and Madagascar (SECAM) assembled a high-level consultation in Nairobi, Kenya. This was to be a serious examination of conscience for the church regarding its responsibility in the events of Rwanda. Ten months later, the Acholi Religious Leaders Peace Initiative (ARLPI) met in Kitgum to begin an interfaith attempt to resolve the slow death of the Acholi people of northern Uganda.

Since then, our struggle has become known to millions of people living in Europe and North America. *Child, Victim, Soldier,* as well as a large number of other books, newspaper articles, magazine articles, DVDs, and videos, have enabled the world to connect to our people. The ARLPI is consoled that many people are hearing in their own tongue about the brutal annihilation that the Lord's Resistance Army is visiting on its own brothers and sisters, a calamity compounded by the Ugandan military. This is the fruit of many advocacy groups and a concrete sign of our solidarity in God's family. How each medium approaches our story is dissimilar, but, nevertheless, there are aspects that seem to be constant.

First, the victims of this horror are the narrators of the story. In this way, it is as if the readers, the listeners, the viewers—as the case may be—hear the sobs and taste the salty tears of their brothers and sisters treated in a most inhumane manner. Second, the very spirituality of the Acholi will vanquish this horror from the land. What do the victims in *Child, Victim, Soldier* tell us? Among other things, we hear about the importance of the *wang oo*—the evening gathering of the extended family around a fire in the middle of the compound outside the grandfather's house. People whose culture is more literate and less oral may overlook the importance of this daily social event because of the pervasiveness of the written word in their life and culture.

In Acholiland, as the sun sets and the work of the day is finished, the extended family gathers. The elders, or let me say, the grandparents, used this special time of the day to pass on by word of mouth their knowledge and the traditions handed down from the ancestors. It is true, as Father Dunson writes: "What was imparted at *wang oo* was expected not only to be listened to seriously by the children but also to be memorized and ultimately interiorized." Like others, I fear that curtailing this beloved tradition for over twenty years because of insecurity has permanently damaged Acholi culture in an irreparable way.

An analogy may help. In my travels and conversations, I have met people researching their roots. If parents and grandparents shared no family history with their children, then, when they died, whatever they knew about the family died with them and their children's research became nearly impossible.

The analogy ceases here, or it would obscure the fact that the Lord's Resistance Army has abducted children. The estimates of abducted children range from thirty to sixty thousand. The rest of the population of Acholiland suffers in Internally Displaced Persons camps (IDP camps). In reality these are death camps, cages in which people are forced to suffer in unspeakable ways. Suicides mount in the camps as mothers are unable to feed their own children. The people and the Acholi culture are dying. The conditions in these camps are inhuman. This tragedy engulfs virtually the entire population—it is the ruination of the Acholi people.

Yet many people, like Father Dunson, who have visited IDP camps experience a profound contrast. Writing of his experience, he says: "In a matter of just two minutes I encounter two contrasting groups of young men. One group appears to have given up on the future; the other is busily planning to embrace it." Caritas International has been working with the second group that Father Dunson encountered. They have received seeds for the next planting, concentrating on onions and tomatoes, and Caritas provided skilled persons who showed them new, more efficient ways of tending to their crops.

The war has shattered the social fabric of hundreds of thousands of families and the rebuilding of family life will require strong leadership. The young people assisted by Caritas could build a new Uganda after this war. So, even from these death camps something good may emerge.

It is the experience of these contrasting groups, I think, that allows one to glimpse obscurely and briefly the spirit and spirituality of the Acholi people. This brings me to my second point: the resolution of this calamity will come from the people. Many different books, articles, and videos report on the fact that the Acholi want to forgive the LRA and celebrate the ritual of forgiveness, a well-established part of Acholi tradition.

As David Lacony tells his story in *Child, Victim, Soldier*, a theme consistent with many other stories across Acholiland emerges, even though the specific details vary. Neighbors, mothers, fathers, and siblings communicate with something as simple as a glance, which indicates to offspring and siblings their permission and their forgiveness—in a real sense, neighbors, mothers, fathers, and siblings have died so that the others might live and hopefully one day escape this nightmare.

The long nightmare of the Acholi has raged for twenty-two years. At this point there is no credible reason to believe that the Ugandan military can totally defeat and destroy the LRA. In the same amount of time, the government of President Yoweri K. Museveni has been unable to restore peace and civility. Nor is there much hope that the international community can realistically achieve the longed-for peace people passionately want.

Concerning Western nations, in her recent book, Kathy Cook wrote that the American nongovernmental organization Human Rights Watch "concluded that the West was less interested in exposing Museveni than in maintaining a good relationship with him." She explained that Museveni is considered by the West to be a crucial leader in the Great Lakes region of eastern and central Africa, a power broker. "Besides," she wrote, "he'd created stability in Uganda and had penned the slogan 'African solutions to African problems,' a slogan the donor countries liked to use to absolve themselves of the mess that colonialism, and later the tactical support of dictators during the Cold War, had left behind." If this analysis proves to be true, then the West has turned a blind eye to the horrifying losses of the Acholi people.

Before the mess colonialism and dictatorships created in Africa, rites of reconciliation brought peace to the African continent. For example, the Nuer and Dinka are seminomadic cattle ranchers neighboring the Acholi to the North. Their rite of reconciliation brought peace to the Nuer and Dinka who were fighting for the same grazing land, a peace that lasted more than 150 years without any fences. The ARLPI resolutely turns to the Acholi tradition, known as *mato oput*.

The rite of reconciliation is an intimate and profound part of the Acholi and its culture. Access to it requires no money. On the other hand, all of the guns, munitions, grenades, and landmines used by both the LRA and the Ugandan military are imported and cost enormous sums of foreign exchange, to which the people do not have access.

This rite of reconciliation holds out the hope of peace, while holding on to guns and munitions means that the Acholi devastation continues. Father Dunson knows that love for one's brothers and sisters needs to be put into action. In his new book, with all his passion and compassion, he has woven together stories of various victims in a way that facilitates reconciliation—the reconciliation that will restore peace to Acholiland.

The Acholi who will emerge from this horrendous guerilla war will be the "new" Acholi. The "old" Acholi I met as a teenager are gone, and much of their life died with them. What has endured this trial by fire? The ability of the people to rise above the inhumanity of the LRA and the Ugandan military and to embrace these fighters in such a way as to heal them of their demons, so that they may once again break bread with us as brothers and sisters.

Archbishop John Baptist Odama
Gulu, Uganda

Introduction

Let there be respect for the earth
Peace for its people
Food for the hungry
Comfort for the poor
Freedom for the downtrodden
Solace for the broken-hearted
Love in our lives
Delight in the good
Forgiveness for past wrongs
And from now on
A new beginning

—Millennium Resolution:
Uganda Martyrs University

My name is Samuel. In the course of my short life all I have ever wanted is enough food to be free from want and a world at peace so my family and I might flourish. These treasures seemed to always elude us. We had tenderness and love in our home, but very little food. The elders in our village remember a time, before the war, when food was plentiful. I long to have lived in a time of peace.

I want to tell you about myself. You should know more about me than just the terror engulfing the final days of my life. I am repelled by the prospect that I might be remembered by how I died and not by how I lived.

Where I lived in northern Uganda, there was a madness that seemed all-pervasive. All around us, the conflict and divisions that reigned supreme placed the youngest and the most vulnerable in the greatest jeopardy. Although our parents never stopped struggling to protect us from the guerilla warfare that encircled our lives, their best efforts failed over and over again. Our government seemed busy with many tasks other than trying to forge peace, and the rest of the world community closed their eyes to us. Perhaps this insane war that targeted children was too bizarre and bewildering a problem to confront. I also harbor suspicions that maybe, in the judgment of some, Africa's children are deemed disposable.

The bonds of family love made life rich for me. I believe that the bond of attachment to those whom we love is the most wondrous gift imaginable. This is, undoubtedly, the best part of being human. I feel that countless other members of our human family, spread across the globe, share this same conviction. It was in the circle of family love that I discovered, at a very young age, that we are all made for communion and friendship. We do not walk alone in this world. My family possessed the gift of knowing how to bring forth the best in me.

Our family home was filled with laughter and play. There was always the unwavering belief that the day would come when this guerilla war, our common enemy, would be destroyed and their efforts would come to an end. We would all welcome together a new day. We were desperately poor, but we knew that we would always have one another.

My family and I do not want pity, instead we plead for solidarity. Visible and invisible ties bind together all of us who share this tiny planet. To build a more humane and peaceful world we will all need to embrace in a new way the ties that bind humanity together. My family and my homeland in northern Uganda have suffered for far, far too long. If you had heard our cries for help perhaps you would have given answer. What I know with certainty is that I possess the same thoughts, I cry and delight to the same feelings, and I yearn for the same peace and security as you. That is why I believe that you would have been a shield of defense for me, if only you had known of my perils.

I died near the beginning of my life, at age fifteen. I died young because I was unwilling to fight in a war that has ravaged my homeland for my entire life. I was conscripted into the Lord's Resistance Army, known by everyone here simply as the LRA. They threw me into hell, the hell that is guerilla warfare. I was kidnapped by rebels when I was just twelve and forced to do unspeakable things. I never wanted to be a soldier. I never wanted to be trained to kill. When I could no longer do the rebels' bidding, I fled and with God's grace guiding me found my way home. The only bright new beginning for me came at my own initiative. I forced myself to have courage enough to escape from the rebel marauders who had kidnapped me from my family but who failed to make me their own.

After my escape, I returned to my home in the village of Ngai in the Gulu district of northern Uganda. For as long as I can remember I have shared a small hut on our family property with my younger brothers Lawrence and James. The night that altered our lives forever began as any other. Everyone in the family shared a meal together as was our custom. Afterward, we gathered around the outdoor fireplace to tell stories. I remained outside with Lawrence and James under the moonlit sky late into the evening. Drowsy and ready for sleep, all three of us eventually entered our hut and fell fast asleep.

The second time the rebels came for me was much worse. This time they also took my two younger brothers. James was barely ten years old and our brother Lawrence had just turned eleven. My brothers and I were always especially close. That December night, my stomach churned as I saw the soldiers tie up my brothers and haul all three of us away. I knew that this would end in sorrow. I had lived with LRA rebels before and I knew firsthand that they could make you do anything, anything at all. This time I had a premonition that I would likely die. What I could never have predicted is that James and Lawrence would be forced to participate in my death.

Close to midnight, young men in uniforms kicked the door to our hut open. We did not panic immediately because we had an older brother who was a member of the Ugandan military. He sometimes arrived home at odd times with his soldier friends. We hoped it was simply our older brother making a dramatic entrance.

My brother Lawrence was the first to sense the danger. When he stepped outside he saw many other village boys all tied up in ropes. When James and I looked out, dread and panic seized hold of us. Our lives changed forever. During the next seven hours we were force-marched nonstop with many other youths. When Lawrence complained that the rope that was tied so tightly around our waists was causing him to bleed, the rebels laughed.

We walked for nearly two days, laden down with loot the rebels had stolen along the way. Lawrence remembered that I had warned him to never show fear or pain—that might incite the rebels to kill you for your weakness. During my first abduction I had seen children summarily executed simply for tears they could not hold back. To avoid showing his pain, Lawrence focused on the comforting images of our home life: the water our mother warmed for us each morning, the aroma of our favorite foods, the softness of our beds, and the image of our parents' faces.

On the second day, after crossing the Aswa River, the worst thing possible came to pass. Commander Katalang was in charge of our brigade. The name *Katalang* means "a large black biting ant with a sharp smell." He was the most feared of the rebel leaders. One of the girls within Commander Katalang's brigade recognized me and knew I was an escapee. As she watched me I grew more and more afraid she would betray me. And she did. She reported me to the commander as a deserter from the LRA. The commander decided that I was to be punished with a slow death in order to teach all the others the danger of trying to escape. Katalang ordered me stripped and then caned mercilessly. I was then left alone the entire day to cry myself hoarse in my excruciating pain. On that day, my last on earth, I learned that dying alone is even worse than dying young. I felt abandoned not just by my family, but by all of humanity.

That night was one of the darkest ever—there didn't even seem to be any stars. Because it was so dark, Lawrence was able to crawl to where I had been left to die. I groaned at the slightest touch as he reached out to me. Warm tears rolled down his cheeks and fell on my broken body. My pain was excruciating but I still had much of my wits about me. I admonished my brother for crying for I knew all too well the price he would pay for his tears. My last words to Lawrence were a soft, nearly inaudible whisper: "Go back to the rest of the group and do whatever the commanders tell you, even if they tell you to kill me. Do it or they will kill both of us. And make sure you tell James."

At first light, a furious Commander Katalang found I was still alive. He ordered all the newly abducted youth to bite me, a teenage traitor, to death. My brother Lawrence gasped out loud at the unthinkable but he also remembered my last words to him about what to do if this moment ever came to pass. He participated with all the others in biting my body until he could no longer recognize that I was his brother. There were so many people biting every inch of my body that I quickly lost consciousness.

It was at that moment that Lawrence most wanted our mother.

She always seemed to know what to do when others were in pain. My younger brother felt that our mother could somehow save all of us from this monstrous evil. It had always seemed to us that nothing could defeat her. Yes, she would know precisely what to do.

The rebels had taken James to sleep in a place away from the others that night. Therefore Lawrence never had the chance to pass on my final instructions. But James saw Lawrence biting me and he took it as a signal that this was what he was supposed to do.

Lawrence's dominant and recurring thought during this unbearable ordeal was that he wished I would open my eyes so that we could see each other one last time. Lawrence bit ever so slightly at my ears to be within my eyesight in case I opened my eyes. He knew my heart and was convinced that I would find great solace in seeing the face of someone I loved at the moment of death.

But I never opened my eyes.

Both Lawrence and James eventually followed my example and dared to escape. They fled the clutches of the LRA on two separate days. The triumphant moment of their childhood was when they first saw each other in a rehabilitation center and realized they had both made it out alive. Today, they are inseparable, just as the three of us had been in the past.

What remembrances will they take into the future from the time in our childhood when we all stepped into hell? Will it be the exhilarating remembrance of their daring escape from that dark place, with God's hand guiding them? Or will it be the nightmarish remembrances of what happened to me and their part in my death?

It is never possible to leave the past behind. No, we carry it with us. I carried my family's love, especially the love of Lawrence and James, on the journey I made from this world to the next.

What will my brothers Lawrence and James carry into their futures and remember about me? Their involuntary participation in my death will likely tower over everything else that happened to them. I fear for them. I suspect they have scars that remain hidden from others, scars that have penetrated deep into their psyches. I dread the thought that my brothers may never heal. No one should ever have to face such dark memories. I do not hold them accountable. They did what I asked them to do because I had seen that there is no escaping the evil of the rebels. Still, it hurt me to see them join in the events that ended my life.

My body has never been found. This saddens my whole family and compounds their grief.

(The events that chronicle the story of Samuel on these pages are all true. What I have added are only the emotions and moral convictions I believe Samuel held. These emotions and convictions have been gathered from all the other children, like Samuel, who were thrown into this LRA war and have lived to tell the rest of the world their stories.)

Letting Humanity Be Our Bond

As a missionary priest working in Uganda, I wept when I first heard the story of Samuel. I had never encountered such inhumanity, nor could I fathom that such brutality would ever be unleashed on children. As I made my way through the war zone of northern Uganda, I heard hundreds of similarly shocking stories from children whose young lives had been shattered by events far beyond their power to control. All of them forcefully revealed one truth that had never been part of my life: the world is a dark and dangerous place for children.

Everything in my life experience seems to have disproved this statement. Growing up in a large, happy family I always felt protected and prized. By day, there was great camaraderie with my five brothers and our friends and we always watched out for one another. Each night our mother would tuck the six of us into bed with a kiss, a prayer, and a gentle touch. Without fail, our father would then enter the room to check on us and to whisper goodnight. Grandmother was last to enter the bedroom to sprinkle her grandchildren and our beds with holy water. The sensation of the cold water on my face was a message that even God was watching over me and gracing my life in unknown ways.

By contrast, in my travels in East Africa I have encountered terrifying perils that engulf children's lives in horrific ways. On our planet, during our watch, children have become the new face of war. The arming of children has become one of the worst evils of the modern world; the existence of child soldiers represents an absolute defeat for humanity. I fear that in the future when only memories of our time remain, others will wonder of us: "How could they have tolerated the brutal, forced conscription of children to kill?" The future will likely question our very humanity.

During the last two decades in conflict-plagued northern Uganda, more than thirty thousand children have been kidnapped from their families and thrown into bloody guerilla warfare. The Lord's Resistance Army, one of the world's most treacherous rebel brigades, opposes the government of Uganda, a landlocked nation in east central Africa. On my annual trips to this largely forgotten war zone, I've chronicled the stories of many abducted youths who have been forced to fight and kill or die if they refuse. They are victims of circumstance, who have suffered greatly as they hear shouts of "Kill, or be killed."

Many of the profoundest lessons of life come to us in story, in narrative. As we listen to the events in the lives of others we gain clarity and insight into our own lives and our place in God's family. We begin to look at the world through the eyes of another person, and gradually, we may also come to see our world through the eyes of the Other. Such solidarity invariably leads to greater compassion on our part, as the God in whom we believe is compassionate.

The narratives of this book tell of tragic episodes in the lives of those who live at a great distance from us. It is possible to dismiss their stories as remote and utterly removed from our experience. But we do this at grave peril to ourselves and to the future of humanity.

It is a fact that extremely vulnerable youth have been kidnapped and placed in a tragic trap that offered little hope for survival. In an instant they lost the companionship of everyone who loved them. They immediately became part of a rebel group that wanted to use them to satisfy its own ends. What unfolded was a tragedy of epic proportions. Direct knowledge of this tragedy bears a moral responsibility for each of us: we must question who we have become as a global family. How frayed are the ties that bind us to one another in the human family if we allowed so many children to be victimized in this way? Each person who reads these narratives should ask, "What resources do I possess to counter the forces of such a monstrous evil that transforms innocent children into efficient killing machines?"

You will come to know these children intimately. You will learn precisely what they endured and how their lives were devoured by malicious persons with greater strength. You will learn how they survived, against all odds, and the price they paid. Their survival has had enormous physical, psychological, and spiritual consequences, and no one can estimate the terrible cost of their moral diminishment. And that is part of the terrible price extracted from the child soldiers of Gulu who were forced to maim and to kill innocent persons. One child soldier who escaped said, "This war has burned a hole in my soul and changed me forever." Moral diminishment is also a price we all pay for living in a world where so many of our children are denied our protection and irreparably harmed as a result.

We remain face-to-face with the perplexing fact that the youth of the LRA are both innocent victims and guilty perpetrators. Still, these children who have had the worst of the world thrown at them will likely capture your heart, as they did mine. As an eyewitness to their plight, I can testify today that it is an impossiblity to turn away from them and remain true to your own best self. I have looked on their faces and searched in their eyes. Before a word is uttered, their bodies and their spirits shout out to all of us, pleading, "Forgive me the evil I have been forced to do." "Protect me." "Love me back into life." Those who have unleashed violence on them not only engaged in murder of their physical bodies but also attempted to kill the souls of the youth abducted into the rebel brigade. It is not surprising at all that some survivors seem to be among the walking dead.

They wait for our answer. It will reveal as much about ourselves as it does about them. I have to ask myself what kind of wisdom and light our Christian faith can bring to bear on the very darkest corners of the universe.

Adam and Eve, our first parents, had a truly original discovery of each other. When first they gazed upon each other, they discovered two irrefutable truths: they knew they were mysteriously different from all other creatures they encountered on the earth and that they were each other's equals. All of Adam and Eve's children have shared in these same God-given treasures that accompany being human. The quest of the LRA to dominate others and its efforts to reduce its captives to animals were destined from the outset to failure. It is simply impossible to step out of humanity, and that is precisely what the LRA rebels asked their captives to do.

The core conviction of our Christian anthropology is that every human being is created *imago dei*, in the very likeness of God. This is stamped on our personhood prior to any achievement or merit of our

own. It is God's free gift that can never be denied or negated. Such dignity cannot be destroyed by anyone, including ourselves. Christian faith compels its adherents to look on all other persons, regardless of whether they are among the guilty or the innocent, not simply with our own eyes and our own feelings. No, it is the perspective of Jesus the redeemer that matters most. Jesus Christ, the only truly innocent person ever to have walked the earth, took upon himself the guilt of us all. He did this from love and solidarity with God's creation.

Pope John Paul II has preached and taught in a most compelling way the solidarity that exists among us who have been graced with the *imago dei*. To the ancient question found in the first book of the Hebrew Scriptures, "Am I my brother's keeper?" (Gen. 4), John Paul gives a resounding yes. In his encyclical *Sollicitudo rei socialis* he describes clearly what solidarity ought to entail for all of us who seek to be faithful. He writes that solidarity "is not a feeling of vague compassion or shallow distress at the misfortunes of so many people, both near and far. On the contrary, it is *a firm and persevering determination* to commit oneself to the common good; that is to say to the good of all and of each individual, because we are all really responsible for all."[1]

This book will probe the bonds of solidarity, both visible and invisible, that join us to one another, and especially to the children who, by victim of circumstance, have had to bear the most crushing burdens in the human family.

Notes

1. Pope John Paul II, *Sollicitudo rei socialis* (December 30, 1987), 38 (italics in original).

1

Meeting the Victims

Every summer since 2001, I have traveled to Africa. Each time I pack my bag I am haunted by an unexplained sense that I am returning home. Since that very first night, dark and dusty, when I landed at Entebbe Airport on the shores of Lake Victoria, I have felt a mysterious connection to the people and places there. I am irresistibly drawn back.

Africa is our birthplace. Every human person alive today can trace his or her history back to the continent of Africa where humanity was born. Everyone's DNA ultimately tells the same story. Scientists engaged in the cutting-edge science of population genetics can take a small scrape of cells from the inside of anyone's cheek and find indisputable, detailed evidence of an ancestral journey—out of Africa to wherever you now live. As knowledge of our common past comes to the fore in ways previously unimaginable, it is now possible to create a family tree for the whole of humanity. Our common past reveals the long-hidden and countless links that bind us to one another.

What does our birthplace look like today? This land of origin, the place where we human beings first said yes to God's marvelous designs for human living, is caught up in a time of utmost peril. Today Africa is populated with hundreds of millions of young and vulnerable members of the human family who face many dangers. Their greatest apprehension stems from a fear that the rest of humanity has forgotten them.

The opposite of love is not hate but indifference. Many young Africans do not worry that the rest of the world might hate them. Their fears are of another kind. They fear that the global population of non-Africans, 86 percent of all persons alive today, are indifferent, that they simply don't care. They wonder what forces, both near and far, have conspired against them that have led to their becoming the forgotten of humanity. As they yearn for a place at the table of life where there is food, medicine, peace, and solidarity with the rest of humanity they sense that they are virtually alone, without allies.

Africa is young. In the majority of Africa's fifty-three nations, half of the entire population is under fifteen. Because infant mortality rates are among the highest on earth, too many babies and their young mothers die in childbirth. Those who survive childhood often do not have a chance as teenagers to attend a good school and unlock a future of promise. The International Labor Organization estimates that perhaps as many as fifty million youths living in sub-Saharan Africa work at menial jobs instead of furthering their education; their hopes to create new and better possibilities for themselves and their families are never realized.

Societal collapse seems immanent in many areas in Africa where conditions are most dire. The HIV/AIDS pandemic has decimated not only the bodies but also the spirits of tens of millions of people. A staggering fifteen million children have suffered the irreplaceable loss of their mother or father or, in the most tragic cases, both parents. That number will likely double in the next decade. Never before in human history have so many children been forced to face their futures without the touch of parental love, the treasure they themselves most value.

Africa is the only continent to produce less food now than it did twenty years ago, which is why so many of Africa's children are hungry. In Asia, the largest and most populated continent, China has managed to cut its proportion of underweight children by more than half. This extraordinary achievement was accomplished in twelve years, from 1990 to 2002, a relatively short period of time. Too many African children are physically stunted: today over a quarter of children under five years are underweight. The extreme poverty felt across the continent is the breeding ground in which diseases such as malaria, tuberculosis, water-borne diseases and parasites, and hunger-related illnesses flourish.

Because severe poverty strikes equally at the body and the spirit, it is also the breeding ground of despair. It is devastating to talk with children who believe that their likely destiny is to die young and to be quickly forgotten.

Hasn't the time come, at long last, to give answer to those who helped bring humanity's treasure to us? Someone among those early

Family life in northern Uganda—beauty in the midst of poverty

human beings in Africa had to be the first to foster learning and living in a community, and someone had to be the first to foster love and solidarity in the human family. Hasn't the time arrived for us to turn back toward Africa, to respond to the people whose ancestors propelled all of humanity forward such a long time ago?

A striking example of the worldwide apathy toward Africa's children is the protracted war in northern Uganda waged by the rebels of the Lord's Resistance Army (LRA). This ravaging assault directed against the youngest in our African homeland reigned unabated while the world stood silent and indifferent. These children have touched me deeply, their painful physical and emotional scars have devastated me, and yet their courage and hope against all odds have lifted me high. Because the LRA rebels specifically targeted children, the vulnerable young ones whom adults move instinctively to protect, why didn't the world community quickly rally to their defense? In a world of instant messaging and twenty-four-hour news service, how can so few people in the northern hemisphere know that thirty thousand Ugandan children have been kidnapped from their families and forced to commit atrocities in the name of the Lord?

The insights of the French cultural critic René Girard are invaluable as we plot a course for our common action in defense of the most vulnerable members of the human family. When I feel in a state of despair from the horrors I have seen unleashed on children, I turn once again to the hope I find in his writings. Girard reminds us that, when viewed in terms of the larger picture, our cultural and social evolution has been moving inexorably in one direction: toward greater protection of the victim. Girard attributes this new sensitivity directly to Christianity. It is the result of the gospel penetrating and transforming lives and awakening many to action in solidarity with victims.

Never before in human memory have the least, the lost, and the left behind occupied the consciousness of humanity as they do today. We are a people deeply aware of the victimization of others, even those who live at a great distance from us in time or place. René Girard writes:

> Our society is the most preoccupied with victims of any that ever was. Even if it is insincere, a big show, the phenomenon has no precedent. No historical period, no society we know, has ever spoken of victims as we do. We can detect in the

recent past the beginnings of the contemporary attitude, but every day new records are broken. We are all actors as well as witnesses in a great anthropological first.

Examine ancient sources, inquire everywhere, dig up the corners of the planet, and you will not find anything anywhere that even remotely resembles our modern concern for victims. The China of the Mandarins, the Japan of the samurai, the Hindus, the pre-Columbian societies, Athens, republican or imperial Rome—none of these worried in the least little bit about victims, whom they sacrificed without number to their gods, to the honor of the homeland, to the ambition of conquerors, small or great.[1]

Each day I pray that Girard is correct in his assessment that our era, more than any other in human memory, is predisposed to hear and respond to the cries of vulnerable victims, yet I remain baffled by the irony and contradictions in his assessment of our era. While we are apparently so deeply conscious of victims, why have we allowed thirty thousand children in one small region of East Africa to be abducted, reduced to commodities, and turned into agents of death? Is it that we are utterly indifferent to certain types of victims? Do we routinely accept a level of misery and hopelessness on the African continent that we would never accept in any other part of the world? Why is this so? What does this say about us as co-bearers of humanity along with our African brothers and sisters?

This book tells the stories of the youngest victims in the human family, who, I believe, possess a preeminent claim to our loving attention. Why do I hold this conviction? Looking into their eyes, I see the eyes of the Christ Child revealed in each. Listening to them and being in their presence, I have come to believe that the gentle Savior lies hidden and helpless in every one of them. Although they may feel worthless and totally undeserving of love, Jesus Christ has chosen to make his home deep within their vulnerability of body and spirit. Within their young bodies and spirits our God yearns to be loved into life. Our God waits for a future that will forever destroy the shame these former child soldiers bear.

These children have endured the sudden loss of everyone and everything they held dear. They have been seized by evil men, often in

the middle of the night, torn from their loving families and supportive communities, and immediately thrown into unimaginable perils. Pressed into lives of perpetual danger, they view each new day as perhaps the last day of their lives. Every moment brings new fears while impending death looms as an ever-present possibility. It is estimated that perhaps as many as ten thousand children are already dead, victims of absurd violence, a brutality whose raw savagery makes it difficult to write or read about.

Can you remember when you were young and walked with innocence, trusting the adult world around you to protect you? These children of war have experienced the shattering of all trust and the loss of all innocence. Gone is any childlike trust or belief that they live in a world that is safe and good. Rather, they sense that something evil will happen to them again, likely sooner than later. They possess a sense of inevitability about it as if it were their inescapable lot.

Why do I travel regularly to northern Uganda to spend my summers among formerly abducted child soldiers? Sunday Obote is the simple answer.

Who Sunday Obote is remains complex and mystifying for me, as I am sure he will be for you. This young man has eyes that can accuse you of neglect while simultaneously pleading for your forgiveness for the unspeakable acts he committed with frightening regularity while in the rebel brigade.

On the afternoon of July 4, 2001, I visited a rehabilitation center for war-traumatized youth in Gulu, a city in northern Uganda. GUSCO, Gulu United to Save the Children Organization, is a holy place where children are literally loved back into life. In GUSCO, more than 7,600 youths have been helped to reclaim their lives from their rebel kidnappers and from bloody ordeals no child should ever see, let alone perpetrate.

I interviewed child psychologists, counselors, and many staff personnel who work with these emotionally fragile children. Since I had not met a single former child soldier, I begged the head administrator to allow me access to one of the former child soldiers for an interview. I was told to sit in the shade of the largest tree on the compound and wait. He sent me a fifteen-year-old boy named Sunday Obote. I was told that he spoke only the Acholi language—fortunately I had a translator with me—and that he had been rescued a short time before.

Nothing in my life prepared me for my encounter with Sunday Obote. After the first minutes of our conversation I knew that I had never looked into the eyes of someone so young and so wounded as this teenager. Nor had I ever met a youth so familiar with killing. As I listened to Sunday, I said to myself, "My God, the world at its worst has been thrown at him!" I knew, almost instantly, that this young man sitting peacefully with me in the shade of that large tree, and smiling whenever I smiled at him, was the most vulnerable person ever to step into my life.

Despite the presence of armed guards at every entrance—so fearful are the youth of reabduction—I felt no physical danger or threat to my person as Sunday relayed stories so filled with terror that they caused me to shiver. A lifetime of feeling safe and protected accompanied me to the war zone.

But I did fear for my soul. My new, firsthand knowledge of the plight of these extremely vulnerable children would bear vast moral consequences. I felt ill prepared to assume them. After this hour with Sunday Obote, how could I not act on his behalf and still remain a disciple of Jesus? I had a haunting suspicion that God was speaking to me through this wounded child who was trying so very hard to hide his pain.

I turn to words of well-known spiritual writer Ronald Rolheiser, a colleague of mine at Louvain, to describe my new friend, who bears for me a startling revelation of Jesus: "What does God's power look like? How does it feel to feel as God in this world? If you have ever been overpowered physically and been helpless in that, if you have ever been hit or slapped by someone and been powerless to defend yourself or fight back, then you have felt how God feels in this world."[2] Since that first conversation with Sunday, I've spent many hours reflecting on the connection between Sunday and Jesus. I have come to a bewildering and growing conviction that Jesus lies hidden and helpless in humanity's extremely vulnerable persons. God's preferential place is to be with those in the human family for whom there is nothing else: no love, no companionship, seemingly no future at all.

Jesus mounted a cross for us as a loving victim. Sunday Obote, stolen from his family as a child and forced to do abominable acts or be killed, is a victim of this world's evil. Jesus, the supreme victim, reveals the plight of all victims. Sunday's eyes provided a glimpse of this truth.

I left this memorable encounter with a renewed conviction that all of humanity is connected and that child soldiers who suffer and die are our children. We share responsibility for them—along with guilt for their plight and accountability for their rescue.

My friend Sunday Obote was just seven years old in 1994 when the Lord's Resistance Army stormed his family home in northern Uganda during the dark of night. The LRA believes that the fighting age begins at seven. That summer night one small boy lost his childhood and all of humanity was diminished in this single act.

For the past two decades the Ugandan rebels have come at night to steal children to swell their ranks. More than 70 percent of this guerilla rebel brigade comprises kidnapped children. Some of these children have been forced to kill a parent or a sibling as part of the abduction plan. The trauma and stigma of the murder leaves the children with the belief that they can never return, that they have lost home forever. Also lost forever are their innocence and their nature as children.

They are warned that if they should escape from the LRA, no one at home will accept them back after what they have done. Once part of the rebel group, they are thrown into the front line of battle, one more concrete expression of how disposable they are to their captors. The war in Uganda is decidedly a war on children. Although Uganda is one of the poorest nations on our planet, it possesses one of the highest birthrates in the world, providing a readily available supply of soldiers-to-be for the rebels. Commodified in this way, Uganda's wonderful resource of children is being decimated by the LRA.

Sunday Obote has written a sketch of his life as part of his healing process and can recount in detail everything that happened to him while in custody of the rebels. Abducted in 1994, during the next eight years he was an eyewitness to the terror committed in the name of the Lord. The only part of his life he remembers fondly is his early childhood. Sunday recalls: "I can remember the time before the rebels abducted me. I was living peacefully in the remote village of Pabbo, about two or three kilometers from the nearest road. With some village children my age, I used to go fishing in a river. I was good at catching fish. Those were happy times. We used simple hooks baited with white ants that we found in anthills in the months of April and May. They are even good food for human beings. Another interesting thing we did was hunting birds. We used slingshots. You had to hide in a bush, as the birds must not see you. Sometimes we would catch a bird, and then we would celebrate with joy and share it among ourselves." This happy time was in stark contrast to the atrocities soon to be unleashed on him and his young companions.

Life turned very dark for Sunday when he was forced into the LRA. He remembers his capture: "On a weekend at midnight everything was quiet. We were four in our grass hut—my mother was there, my sister Christine, my brother Joseph, and myself. Suddenly the door was kicked open and men in army uniforms with torches entered the hut. They ordered us to sit. Some were busy removing whatever valuables we had. They said Joseph and I should show them the way back to the road. They told my mother that we would come back soon. It was all a trick."

For the next eight years Sunday endured the daily savagery of life in the LRA. The worst ordeal was unquestionably the first killings. In a calculated way the rebels worked to destroy the human instincts of these young children in order to turn them into efficient killing machines ready to strike on command.

Sunday tells of that first day in captivity. "When we reached the road we joined a bigger group. There were about fifty children our age. The next morning, Odocki, one of the children, tried to escape. He was recaptured by the guards posted half a kilometer from the spot where we spent the night. This was the scariest thing I saw. Odocki was brought before us all. The commander said: 'I will prove to you that we don't like children who try to escape. This boy will die in front of you here because he tried to escape.' Odocki was then hit on the head with a big axe. He was dead but they continued to hit him until you could not recognize he was human. We were warned not to cry for him."

After the first deadly blow, why did the rebels continue their heinous assault on the dead body of Odocki? To destroy the humanity of Sunday and all the other new recruits, who were forced to witness the murder of this innocent boy without shedding a tear. Tears are a sign of both the natural innocence and the weakness of children. The first requirement of the boy soldier is that he be free of innocence and weakness in order to gain the ability to kill on command. The boys were programmed to become unfeeling, killing machines, a mere extension of their gun or machete. The first step in the process was to obliterate the distinctively human attributes of the boys. Sympathy, compassion, and a natural proclivity to connect with other persons in jeopardy are actions that belong innately to human beings. And it is in the nature of children to cry when they are hurt or when they see someone else who is hurt; it is not in their nature to strike the vulnerable other. Emotions such as compassion must be quickly destroyed if the new recruit is to become a valuable member of the LRA. So Sunday did not cry when Odocki was murdered out of the sheer fear of reprisal and the knowledge that what happened to Odocki could happen to him if he did not follow each rebel order.

Although Sunday had been told to forget his past, this was the first rebel command he refused to obey. In an act of internal defiance against his captors, Sunday memorized the image of his mother's face, the face of love, and kept it constantly before him. He was not willing to step into his future without this treasure. This alone could bring him comfort, and he knew that no one could enter into his mind and heart and see what he had hidden there. Love would remain intact.

Through the savage killing of Odocki and other equally brutal actions, Sunday and the other newly abducted recruits learned that unswerving allegiance to the group was demanded. Conformity to the will of the rebel leaders was stressed at each moment of the day. No personal emotions were allowed. Feelings of empathy for other children in particular had to be crushed.

The boys were trained in the use of weapons and told that their guns were now "their mothers, their best friends, their everything." The young girls who had been kidnapped were given to the commanders as trophies for their military victories. All these girls routinely suffered sexual abuse at the hands of men who treated them as their personal playthings. Nine out of ten girls who were lucky enough to be rescued from the LRA by the Ugandan People's Defense Force (UPDF), or who managed to escape, fled with a sexually transmitted disease, often HIV.

At the time Sunday was captured, the LRA maintained its main camp in southern Sudan, where the LRA leader, Joseph Kony, was taking safe haven. After military threats and demands for surrender, the LRA had moved there in 1994 with the approval of Sudanese officials. Once in the hands of the LRA, the abducted children were often taken to this base of operation for further training and indoctrination into the life of a child soldier. The rebels were without any means of transportation, so the arduous journey was made on foot by the thousands of children they abducted.

The march north from Uganda to southern Sudan caused even greater suffering for the children, who knew that their only chance to stay alive was to please their captors in every way. Sunday described the march: "Some children became too tired to walk and simply fell down on the ground. We were then ordered to beat them to death. Imagine a line of two or three hundred people all beating one fallen child. The last persons in the line would beat nothing but scattered pieces of a human body. Although we were forced to participate we would always remember exactly who had been killed. All those years I witnessed many such killings."

For Sunday, as for each of us, it is hard to face the dark truths about ourselves and claim ownership of our wrongdoing, especially when grave evil is involved and we know there will be devastating consequences—to ourselves and to others. When Sunday told me he was writing a journal to record exactly what had happened in the bush I was exuberant. Many times before I have seen how journaling can make pain tolerable, how confusion can give way to clarity, and how character can be made stronger. I sensed it could be a major help in the healing process for Sunday.

In our ongoing conversations—and we've talked together often since our first meeting in 2001—I am often struck by a sense that Sunday saw himself principally as a witness to all this graphic violence. Accepting even his forced role in these many killings was an altogether unresolved matter. In his journal it was not uncommon to find such sentences as, "All those years I witnessed many such killings." This is in no way an accurate description of his life with the rebels. He was not only a witness; he participated directly in grotesque and bizarre killings so raw in their fury that it's extremely troubling to imagine him doing such things.

I often think about how Sunday has distanced himself from these horrific acts of violence, acts he was forced to perform. Sunday's detachment from the killings he engaged in brought to my mind the ancient Greek story of Orestes, a tale of another youth caught up in the act of killing. The mother of Orestes, Clytemnestra, takes a lover and together with her lover murders her husband, Agamemnon. The Greek code of honor at the time demanded that a son avenge the killing of his father, but in this case, his own mother was involved.

Orestes killed his mother and his mother's lover, thus avenging his father's death. But the gods cursed him with the Furies, three ghastly harpies, who tormented him and drove him to the brink of madness. For years and years Orestes roamed the land seeking to atone for his crime, continually pursued by the Furies. Finally, he petitioned the gods to lift the curse.

A form of trial was held in which the god Apollo spoke on behalf of Orestes. Apollo argued that, after all, Orestes bore little responsibility for his crime of matricide because the Greek code of honor had demanded that he exact revenge. Further, Apollo argued that he himself had actually engineered the situation that placed Orestes in the terrible predicament of having to kill. At this, in one version of the myth, Orestes promptly fired Apollo as his spokesperson and stood up to speak on his own behalf. He said: "I did it. I killed my mother and my mother's lover."

Never before had an individual so fully accepted responsibility for his actions instead of seeking to blame another. The gods were pleased with Orestes and lifted the curse of the Furies. The Furies were transformed into the Eumenides, loving spirits to offer Orestes counsel and comfort all his days. Orestes found healing and new beginnings only when he fully faced the truth about himself—no matter how dark, disappointing, or shameful that truth was.

I worry about my young friend Sunday. Accepting responsibility is often a key, decisive component to stopping a cycle of violence and destruction. When no one claims the power to stop the violence, a profound hopelessness takes root. Denials feed on themselves until persons are left utterly unable or unwilling to see the truth about themselves and their world.

As a priest, I frequently visit prisons and many times I have witnessed the life-changing moment when, after years of burying the truth, a person finally accepts responsibility for a horrendous action. There is a cleansing and freeing of the spirit that accompanies such brutal honesty. A new beginning is born in that moment of accountability and truth.

In the summer of 2006, I visited a maximum-security prison in East Africa. I was asked to visit and counsel prisoners who had committed capital crimes and faced either execution or a lifetime of imprisonment. One man related to me how he came home early one afternoon and found a naked man in his bed with his wife. The naked man dashed away in fear as the husband chased after him. Unable to stop him, the enraged husband went home and beat his wife. Two days later she died.

Until then this man had never hurt a single human being. Now he had to face the devastating fact that his first act of violence was to kill the person he loved most. His punishment goes well beyond a lifetime in prison; he told me he grieves every hour for the loss of his young wife. He mourns not only for his personal loss, but also for all the good his wife would have done in this world had he not succumbed to his rage. Each day he bears the knowledge that his actions have left their small children without parents to rear them.

What I find remarkable is the grace that brought this man the moral courage and the insight to judge his own behavior. He was able to recognize and name the evil he succumbed to, and he deeply, profoundly regretted his actions. This war on children in northern Uganda has raged on in large measure because no one has been willing to take responsibility for forging a new way forward, and no one has been willing to accept responsibility for this failure. This is the crux of the moral dilemma that plagues this region of the world.

To achieve inner peace and lay out clear goals for his life, I believe that Sunday must face his own past, with all its demons, with the same kind of radical honesty and ownership of his actions.

The plight of the thousands of children like Sunday Obote who have been brutalized by the LRA has received scant attention in North America. In 2003 at a press conference in Nairobi, Jan Egeland, the UN Under-Secretary-General for Humanitarian Affairs, referred to the chaos in northern Uganda as the largest neglected humanitarian emergency in the world. In 2004, he asked world leaders, "Where else in the world have there been more than 20,000 kidnapped children? Where else in the world has 90 percent of the population in large districts been displaced? Where else in the world do children make up 80 percent of the terrorist insurgency movement?" Nowhere.

Since that July afternoon in 2001, Sunday has become part of my life, like a son to me. His own father was slain by the LRA when he was still a toddler. We correspond regularly, and I provide for his education, food, and housing. His primary concern is still his security, so that he can once again feel safe in his homeland.

I return regularly to East Africa to check on Sunday's progress and to meet his new friends. His best friend is a twenty-five-year-old named John Kennedy. (Ugandans like to name their children after famous Americans.) I also met Richard Nixon, another twenty-five-year-old Ugandan. John Kennedy was also abducted by the LRA and spent seven weeks in captivity before he escaped. They share the experience of the LRA, although Sunday spent seven years in captivity before his rescue. Life holds many dangers for these Ugandan youth.

Sunday continues to fear abduction and insists on living far from his family. Robbed of his childhood education, Obote, now in his early twenties, is in the fourth grade. It is awkward and challenging for him to sit in a classroom full of much younger children, but he knows that education is the only key to unlocking his future. He is six feet tall so he always sits in the last seat in the back of the classroom so he won't obstruct anyone's view of the blackboard or the teacher.

The challenges Sunday Obote faces go beyond the endurance of many of us, but I am still filled with hope for his future. Hope grew from my very first conversation with him. At the time, he was staying at GUSCO and spending several months in rehabilitation so he could eventually rejoin his family and community. As that first conversation drew to a close, Sunday said to me with near glee in his voice, "Do you know that there are people here who love me?" Then a teenager who had lost his entire childhood and its innocence to one of the world's great evils, he had not failed to remember what love is. This, I suspect, is the source of his resilience.

That day, captured in Sunday Obote's personal journey out of the evil of war, I saw a timeless truth. It is the truth that St. Paul revealed to us in the First Letter to the Corinthians: the power and the tenacity of love, its supremacy in this world, are beyond our imagining. Sunday is the concrete embodiment of the power of love to endure. It can outlast anything, including a childhood lost to guerilla warfare in which death stalks during each moment of the day and night. Sunday's image of his mother's loving face was one singular comfort; it touched him before his captivity and it gave him a reason to believe in the future.

Love still stands when all else has fallen.

Notes

1. René Girard, *I See Satan Fall Like Lightning* (Maryknoll, NY: Orbis Books, 2001), 161.

2. Ronald Rolheiser, *The Holy Longing: The Search for a Christian Spirituality* (New York: Doubleday, 1999), 186-87.

2

The Background of the LRA Rebellion

L ush landscapes, offering an almost Eden-like panorama, are one of
the reasons that Sir Winston Churchill called Uganda the "Pearl
of Africa." Its stunning natural beauty stands in stark contrast to
the genocide, war, and hunger that have doggedly plagued this region
of East Africa for more than half a century.

The ongoing civil strife in northern Uganda is a complex web of
historical, cultural, and tribal factors that are frequently overlooked or
simplified. Fully disentangling them is not possible; all contributed in
ways small or great to the present turmoil. The seeds of division were
beginning to be sown more than a century and a half ago.

In the 1800s the "Scramble for Africa" was under way. Many
European nations, hungry for African resources, were vying with one
another for dominance. In this sub-Saharan region of the continent
Belgium took the Congo, Great Britain received the largest segment of
Africa including Kenya and Uganda, while Germany laid claim to the
right to colonize Tanzania and Rwanda. After Germany was defeated
in World War I, the League of Nations gave Rwanda to Belgium to
administer. There are striking parallels between the way Belgium colonized Rwanda and Britain colonized Uganda.

The Belgian rule was neither just nor impartial. From the outset,
the Belgian colonizers favored members of the Tutsi tribe over the
Hutu. The Tutsi were taller, of slimmer stature, and lighter in color,
the more European-looking of the native inhabitants. There was a kind
of preferential option "for people who look like us." The Europeans
saw the Tutsi in a most favorable way. They were invited to become
the enforcers of Belgian rule while the Hutu were viewed as the work
force. This favoritism helped fuel the animosity and hatred that would
eventually explode into genocide at the end of the twentieth century.

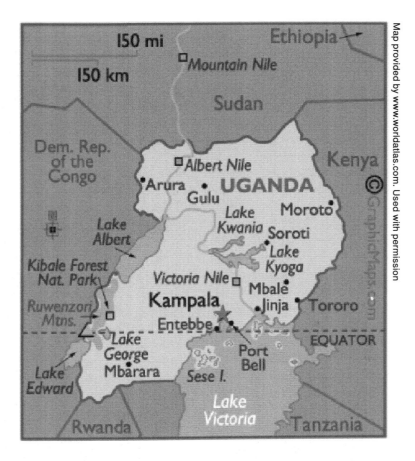

150 mi

150 km

Ethiopia

□ Mountain Nile

Sudan

Dem. Rep.
of the
Congo

□ Albert Nile

Kenya

UGANDA

• Arura   • Gulu

Lake
Kwania

Moroto

Lake
Albert

Soroti
• Lake
Kyoga

Kibale Forest
Nat. Park

Victoria Nile □

Mbale

Ruwenzori
Mtns.

□

Kampala

Jinja

Tororo

Entebbe

EQUATOR

Lake
George

Port
Bell

Lake
Edward

Mbarara

Sese I.

Rwanda

Lake
Victoria

Tanzania

The Hutu and Tutsi, in 1994, began to slaughter each other, resulting in the unimaginable suffering and deaths of nearly three-quarters of a million people in just three months.[1]

The European notion that certain tribes or races were born to rule and that others were born to be ruled over has long weighed down this region of Africa.

In the 1860s British explorers who were traversing east central Africa in search of the source of the Nile River spurred British interest in this area. In 1894 Britain established a protectorate, encompassing various ethnic groups in east central Africa, that later became Uganda. British "divide and rule" colonialism helped to fuel tensions between the tribes, thus helping to assure Britain's ascendancy over all.

The dominant southern Bantu tribe was given economic, political, and educational advantages by their British colonizers. The British form of favoritism fueled some of the same destructive results as Belgian favoritism: primarily enmity between the tribes. The northerners, members of the Acholi, Langi, Madi, Kakwa, and Alur tribes, were recruited principally for the military, for positions within the police, and for a host of jobs in manual labor, particularly on the many sugar plantations the British established in Uganda.

Over time, British colonial leadership played on these divisions and often exacerbated them to their own political advantage. Indeed, the British deliberately stifled education in the north, and associated prospects for employment, so that the entire region would remain a steady source of military recruits and manual laborers. As a direct result of the advantages given to the Bantu tribe, their homeland in southern Uganda grew far more prosperous than the north.

Tribalism, with its enduring tribal rivalries, remains strong across the African continent. This is especially true in Uganda where it has remained a long-standing tradition and is engrained into political and cultural life. Many people self-identify first as a member of a particular tribe, not simply or principally as Ugandans. One Acholi government official told me that the greatest punishment, feared more than the death penalty, is to be expelled from the tribe.

Those in political and economic power are known to favor members of their own tribe in filling positions of influence in both civil and economic structures. Over the short span of time since Ugandan independence in 1962, Ugandan national leaders have often promoted those with ethnic and cultural links to themselves, again sowing the seeds of bitter resentment.

Tribal rivalry and camaraderie is simply a fact of life in Africa that is little understood outside the continent. At the end of 2007, in neighboring Kenya, the presidential election was marred by tribalism turned into deadly violence, with around one thousand dead in the first weeks. The results of this election, the closest ever held in Kenya, were highly disputed. Some 98 percent of the Kikuyu tribe voted for their own, the incumbent president Mwai Kibaki. The vast majority of Luo tribe members voted for their own, the opposition leader Raila Odinga. With the fiercely contested election results in dispute, tribal militias attacked each other. The bloodshed exposed tribal resentments that have long festered in Kenya. Most of the dead were from President Kibaki's tribe. The Kikuyu tribe comprises only 22 percent of the Kenyan population but they have dominated business and politics countrywide since Kenyan independence in 1963. This has long stirred resentment from the roughly forty other ethnic groups and tribes in Kenya. Many Kenyans, fearful of the postelection bloodletting, fled across the border to Uganda.

After independence from Britain in 1962, Milton Obote became Uganda's first president. Obote, a member of the northern Langi tribe, inherited the colonial army with its high percentage of Acholi and Langi. Obote's presidency lasted nine years, during which time he promoted the military career of a then little known colonel named Idi Amin Dada. Amin began aggressively recruiting more and more soldiers from his own West Nile region of northern Uganda and amassing power, causing Obote to feel threatened. Their rift would eventually lead to Obote being overthrown in a military coup led by Amin, who would prove to be Uganda's most brutal and infamous leader.

Amin dissolved the parliament, amended the constitution to grant himself absolute power, and then attempted to militarize Uganda. He immediately went about placing military tribunals above the civil law and appointing many top soldiers to high-level government posts. He renamed Government House, the presidential residence in the capital city, Kampala, "The Command Post." The very leader who had promised the world that he would disband President Obote's secret police established the State Research Bureau, the SRB. Headquartered in

Nakasero, a suburb of Kampala, the SRB came to be known across the globe as a secret, secluded scene of torture and execution.

Massive human rights violations were to follow. It is estimated that more than one hundred thousand people lost their lives during Amin's reign of terror, with most of the dead being members of the Acholi and Langi tribes. Although a northerner himself, a member of the Kakwa tribe, Amin feared the influence of the Acholi and the Langi. One of the chief reasons why Ugandans of the north bore the brunt of Amin's political persecution was because they had supported Milton Obote. As northern Ugandans died in great numbers, the victims of powerful political forces unleashed against them, a deep-seated animosity took hold.

One summer night, while volunteering at a Ugandan orphanage outside the capital city, I observed more than a hundred young boys viewing a film on the life of former president Idi Amin. It was the Saturday evening entertainment that the children looked forward to all week. One episode in the movie depicted President Amin ordering the execution of a Supreme Court justice who refused to do his bidding. Amin arrived at the autopsy and promptly ordered all persons to clear the room. He then proceeded to cut into the slain jurist, remove an organ, and begin to eat of the body of his dead rival. All the children screamed out in disgust. This was a moment when these Ugandan youths were face-to-face with their nation's heritage of militarism and barbarism.

Amin himself was ultimately ousted by a coalition of forces that included Ugandan rebels fighting in a guerrilla brigade known as the National Resistance Army (NRA), made up of supporters of former president Milton Obote and Tanzanian government forces. After Amin's ouster, an interim presidency followed until Milton Obote was restored to power. Obote's return to power also restored the Acholi and the Langi's dominance within the military, while at the same time ushering in one of the bloodiest times in modern Ugandan history.

Endeavoring to stamp out the insurgency movement of the NRA under the leadership of Yoweri Museveni, the army of Obote engaged the NRA in battle north of Kampala in a region known as the Luwero Triangle. The massacre that took place at Luwero has no parallel in modern Ugandan military history. The International Committee of the Red Cross estimated that the fighting in the Luwero Triangle led to several hundred thousand dead. As is the case when the homeland is the battlefield, the majority of the dead were civilians.

Museveni's army eventually prevailed, and in 1986, Museveni himself became Uganda's longest-standing leader, remaining as president in power until the present.

Self-serving and despotic leadership has been the rule in Uganda. The legacy of both Presidents Milton Obote and Idi Amin Dada left Uganda virtually in ruins. Uganda was run into the ground with autocratic governing shrouded in concealment, swift and severe police action, and torturous treatment of anyone believed to be a threat to the current regime. To this very day there has never been a peaceful transition of power in modern Uganda.

Many Acholi soldiers, retreating north to Acholiland and into southern Sudan, feared that Museveni would seek revenge on them for the terrible loss of life at Luwero. It was these defeated soldiers who formed the nucleus of the initial rebel brigade that would become the LRA and would fight the government of President Museveni for the next two decades. Their first leader was a most improbable choice: a female prophetess who wanted to put right the cruel grievances of her people.

On January 2, 1985, an Acholi woman named Alice Auma claimed that a spirit had taken possession of her that day. The spirit was known as *Lakwena* ("messenger" in Acholi) and she became known thereafter simply as Alice Lakwena. That experience gave birth to a powerful prophetic movement that met with major successes in a dazzling attempt to topple the Ugandan government. Her authority came from the "spirit" that possessed her, and tens of thousands of Acholi came to believe in her supernatural powers.

Alice, with the authority of one who wants to rule with "higher powers," raised an army called the Holy Spirit Mobile Forces. Her rebel brigade eventually reached as far south as Jinja. Alice Lakwena's seven thousand hymn-singing fighters reached within sixty miles of the capital city, Kampala, before being defeated by the Ugandan People's Defense Force (UPDF) in 1988. This Acholi prophetess led the most successful military insurrection ever against President Museveni and his government.

Why do people follow self-proclaimed prophets? Alice began her career as a highly successful faith healer who captured the imagination of the Acholi people. Over time, the Acholi came to believe that God's providence had also sent the Lakwena because Museveni wanted to kill all the Acholi male youths. The Acholi leaders surmised: "What good is it to cure a man today only that he be killed tomorrow by his own government?" They determined that God must have been asking Alice to stop the bloodshed before continuing her work as a doctor-healer.

For Alice, her dual roles as healer and military leader were closely interwoven. Alice had promised to heal the Acholi of the evil spirits and witchcraft that had plagued Acholi life and brought down the wrath of God. With the aid of her forceful and very charismatic personality, Alice convinced her soldiers that they had to be purified before they could usher in a new era of peace and prosperity. Drinking alcohol, abusive language, stealing, smoking tobacco, and all forms of quarreling were strictly forbidden.

Acholiland is a bastion of magical thinking. Alice Lakwena adamantly demanded that every soldier undergo initiation rites in which they burned their old clothes, symbolic of their leaving behind the old ways of life, which often included sorcery or witchcraft. In a ritual shockingly similar to Christian baptism, their bodies were anointed with shea oil for protection from all that harms. Alice promised her fighters that the use of her "holy oil" would protect them from the enemy, turning the bullets of the enemy into water. Alice taught that those who died in the gunfire were weak of faith. While she demanded her followers to abandon false spiritual and magical beliefs, she filled them with ever more fanciful and imaginary beliefs that suited her purposes.

Alice's army did not have the benefit of modern instruments of warfare. The UPDF soldiers were, on the other hand, equipped with machine guns and artillery fire. Lakwena gave her fighters sticks, stone grenades, and machetes, demanding that none of her soldiers ever attempt to take cover from the enemy even if they approached with far superior weaponry. That was a sign of disloyalty and lack of belief in the higher powers that would give them their victory. Alice instructed her soldiers that all their trust needed to be in the higher spiritual powers that could do for them what they could not do for themselves. For example, she taught that their stone grenades, when hurled toward the enemy in combination with holy water, created a force field of protection for the Holy Spirit Mobile Forces.

The false illusion of invincibility that Alice built up led her soldiers to be far more daring, to take ever-greater risks. In the short term this proved extraordinarily successful. Stunning victories were won early on with this strategy as thousands of poorly equipped soldiers simply would not stop marching forward. The UPDF soldiers were taken by surprise by this extraordinary way of engaging in battle. In the end, superior technology won the day, but Alice's victories were already taking on legendary status as her military successes were told and retold across East Africa.

When Alice saw countless numbers of her soldiers dead on the battlefield at Jinja, she knew immediately that her quest for military victories was forever over. She saw that there was no alternative for her but to flee into exile. She went to Kenya, where she remained in relative obscurity until her death in 2007. The bloody losses sustained by Lakwena's fighters were the heaviest loss of African life involving magical belief and warfare since the Maji-Maji revolt in 1904 and 1905.

Joseph Kony—Mystifying Madman

Upon the devastating defeat and abrupt departure of Alice Lakwena, a twenty-five-year-old Acholi man named Joseph Kony suddenly came to prominence in northern Uganda. He took up the mantle of those in the Acholi tribe who remained fixed on a military victory as the only possible solution to the ongoing turmoil afflicting their homeland. While always claiming that he was a freedom fighter and not a terrorist, Kony nonetheless became accustomed to ordering the terrifying mutilations of countless persons. Massacres ensued on his command. Children suffered in previously unimaginable proportions.

Kony is a man of mystery. He appears to many to be both a mystic and a madman. Pictures of him are rare. Few outside the LRA have ever even met him. One fact about the life and activities of Joseph Kony is indisputable. He is a known expert in manipulating and exerting extraordinary power over young and pliable children while remaining an elusive, hunted man. Indeed, he may be Africa's most wanted man.

Kony seems to have made it his life's ambition to remain elusive. His whereabouts are almost always impossible to confirm, which has served him well on many fronts. For the past two decades the Ugandan military has been desperately attempting to kill him, to no avail. The International Criminal Court (ICC) in The Hague has issued no less than thirty-three charges against him, including murder, sexual enslavement, pillaging, and the forced abduction of children into guerilla warfare. As a result of this action by the ICC, one hundred and five nations have pledged to arrest him if he steps foot into their jurisdiction.

Kony has a critical sense for predicting danger and fleeing from it. His current address is likely the Garamba Forest, located in the eastern region of the Democratic Republic of the Congo. This area is one of the most impenetrable regions of East Africa, located in one of the more highly unstable nations in the world community. The deadly violence in the Congo is the bloodiest within any single nation since the end of World War II, with an estimated five million people dead. The most unstable region of the Congo today is the east, where Kony hides. Kony must surely sense he is safe there, since currently lawlessness reigns supreme.

Joseph Kony asserts that he has always had only one goal. He has claimed repeatedly that all he intends is to establish the biblical Ten Commandments as the rule of law for his fellow Ugandans. Few have been won over to this claim. Kony himself violates each of the commandments in his unbridled, inordinate pursuit of power at any cost. Originally, the band of soldiers Kony gathered around him, mostly the remnants of Alice's army, were called the United Holy Salvation Army, or simply the UHSA. He has always claimed that he was a freedom fighter, a man in search of salvation for himself and for his compatriots. Others call him a terrorist and a mass murderer. On December 5, 2001, the U.S. Department of State placed his rebel group, the Lord's Resistance Army, on its list of known terrorist operatives.

Supreme Commander Joseph Kony sees it another way. He claims to be waging war based on a direct summons from God. Kony tells everyone that God speaks directly to him. God alone has instructed him and has entrusted to him a task given to no one else. He is to replace the Ugandan government of President Yoweri Museveni with a government more pleasing to the divine, based on the biblical Ten Commandments, with Kony himself at the helm.

When Joseph Kony first appeared in person at a series of peace talks that failed in 1994, robed men sprinkling holy water preceded his entrance. By this, and other such ritualistic actions, Joseph Kony has carefully orchestrated a presentation of himself as a holy crusader. He wants the rest of the world to see that he has embraced a noble cause, a crusade blessed by our God, who has required of Kony daring and decisive measures.

Wherever Kony set up camp, he always had a shrine built for him to commune with the divine spirit. When he was "praying," he might change his voice or feign losing consciousness. He would suddenly shout out messages that a scribe would be required to record and relay to Kony's lieutenants. One message was, "Thirty people should be killed." After receiving that message his soldiers followed the instruction precisely as dictated and indiscriminately killed thirty persons. Kony's words are viewed as gospel and law in the LRA.

The leader of the LRA has always carefully crafted a cultic mystique around his person. This has been done deliberately as part of an overall strategy to convince the young and the impressionable that all of Kony's actions are filled with integrity and religiosity. Kony self-identifies with such actions as the sprinkling of holy water, yet the orders he gives to his soldiers could never be accompanied by the descriptive word *holy*. He orders the unleashing of misery and abominations one would think human beings incapable of performing. Oddly, it appears that Kony himself does not kill: he only incites others to deadly menace and to the fraying of all the ties that bind humanity together. He orders others to kill in a strategic way, a way that has kept him in a very powerful place of dominance for over two decades.

In 2006, the former BBC correspondent Anna Borzello was able to interview the LRA leader. This alone was a feat since Kony guards his privacy as much as he guards his protection. It was understood by many Ugandans that Kony now found it expedient to tell the world his version of the story of the LRA. He was hoping that some in the world community could still be won over to his version of events. In that interview, Joseph Kony made an amazing claim. He stated: "*I am a human being, just like you.*" This simple statement, which reveals so much about this eccentric warlord, repulsed me.

As I read an account of that interview and was stunned by Kony's assertion, I immediately called to mind Robert Antelme's captivating work *The Human Race*.[2] The only book he wrote, it is autobiographical in nature and chronicles his deportation from Paris by the Gestapo in June of 1944. He was hauled away, much like the victims of this LRA war, into the inhumanity found in the concentration camps at Buchenwald, Gandersheim, and finally Dachau. While he was brutalized in every seemingly inhuman way by the Nazis, he never ceased to be aware that his tormentors, who sought to deprive him of his distinctively human qualities, were themselves human beings. That cannot be said of Joseph Kony, the tormentor and the victimizer. He sought to obliterate the humanity of the children he had taken captive.

There is a very precise and compelling reason why Joseph Kony is wanted by the International Criminal Court in The Hague for crimes against humanity. It is because what he has done is an assault upon us all. It is because Joseph Kony's actions are not the actions of a human being like us. Indeed, they are intended, rather, to kill us and to destroy the ties that bind together the human family. That is why the global community of nations agreed that he must be stopped and brought to justice.

Kony has never been as popular with the Acholi people as Alice Lakwena. Therefore, he felt compelled to use coercion, abduction, and terror to build his army, while Alice had built her forces on the sheer magnetism of her personality. Joseph Kony unleashed the worst reign of terror—the likes of which the Acholi have never known—and a misery unlike anything they had experienced, even under the feared dictator Idi Amin Dada.

Child Abductions Increase

Child abductions in northern Uganda rapidly accelerated in 2002. From June 2002 until June 2003 some 8,400 youths were captured by the LRA in only twelve months, more than in any previous year. The screams and the dreadful cries of Ugandan mothers and fathers without their children rang out across northern Uganda that year unlike any other year in this young East African nation's history. A terrible sadness took hold of many families then as the absence of beloved daughters and sons was felt in thousands of households.

Until 2002, the LRA had been principally based in southern Sudan, conducting cross-border raids to pillage the Acholi villages and to abduct Acholi youth. This could never have been realized without the support of the government of Sudanese President Omar al Bashir. Sudan claimed that the Ugandan government was supporting the efforts of the Sudanese People's Liberation Army (SPLA). The SPLA had been in a protracted civil war with the forces of President Omar al Bashir. As retaliatory measures, the Sudanese gave money, weapons, food provisions, and safe haven to the LRA in southern Sudan. Two nations who share a border, in a sometimes-hostile relationship with each other, were channeling support to each other's enemy. Who would first fall victim to this political strategy? The women and the children, the vulnerable civilian population, were the first to feel the brunt of this cruelty. It was not until late 1999 that the governments of Uganda and Sudan entered into an agreement to cease support for each other's rebel groups. Improved diplomatic relations between the two countries led to Sudan giving permission to the Ugandan government to conduct a military operation within southern Sudan to flush out the rebels. This military initiative, known as Operation Iron Fist, resulted in sending ten thousand Ugandan soldiers into southern Sudan.

Nongovernmental organizations that work in Uganda with former child soldiers report that the average age of abductees continued to get younger and younger as the conflict drew on. In the 1990s the LRA targeted youths in their teens, often in the age span between thirteen and seventeen. In the 2000s more and more children who were barely nine or ten were being kidnapped, both boys and girls. The counselors and psychologists at the rehabilitation centers speculate that the chief reason the LRA sought their captives at a younger and younger age is that a younger child is far easier to control and manipulate. An added reason is that younger girls are less likely to be infected with the HIV virus. The rebels who desperately seek "safe" sex slaves, a prized commodity, prefer very young girls. What we know for certain is that the age of the victims of this bizarre war became steadily younger and younger with the passing of each year.

Children have a diminished capacity to distinguish right from wrong, especially in the crisis arena of war. They will frequently do what they are ordered to do by adults in authority over them, sometimes even without hesitation, when responding to a commanding voice. Young persons more easily blur the lines between reality and make-believe, between adventurous games and the finality and severity of deadly pursuits. The LRA seeks to wield astonishing, absolute power over the young and impressionable whom they kidnap to do their bidding, and they often succeeded.

While each child soldier's story is unique, there are areas of commonality. For almost all of them, a day or two after their kidnapping they undergo a rite of initiation. First they are beaten, purportedly to teach them that the life of a soldier is difficult and includes much pain. This clearly serves to communicate to the young recruits that this is the life they can expect. Mark, a seventeen-year-old from Pader district, describes for us what precisely happens: "They gave us 150 strokes of the cane, and eight slaps with the machete on the back. It was the soldiers who did the beatings. For the cane we were made to lie on our stomach and then the soldiers would beat us on the buttocks. There were twenty-three of us. For the machete, we were made to bend over at the waist, and then the soldiers would use the blunt end of it to beat us on the back." The children are told not to cry during their ordeal. Threatened with death should they cry, those who succumbed to the emotion of the moment are clubbed on the back of the head and simply killed.

After it is made clear that their future includes much pain, their bodies are then anointed with shea nut oil in a ritual, like that of Alice Lakwena, that seems a horrible parody of Christian baptism. Not only are their heads anointed in the shape of the Lord's cross, but also their chests, backs, and hands and feet. Each anointing is done in the shape of the cross of Jesus Christ, as if to say that God himself wills their service now, that they belong to a liberation movement that will free their country from tyranny.

The newly anointed are told that through this ritual action they no longer belong to their mother or father—but now and forever belong to the LRA. This anointing is not to assuage the pain from the earlier beatings to their bodies. No. Their rebel captors tell the new child soldiers that the shea nut oil will make it easier for the LRA to locate them should they try to run away. In 2003 a young boy named Samuel told Human Rights Watch that immediately after he was anointed with the shea nut oil the first words his rebel brothers spoke to him in welcome were: "This oil we place upon your body today will help us track you down if you ever dare to escape." A warm welcome indeed!

These children have been made to endure the world at its worst. They have known the sudden loss of everyone they have ever loved, constant hunger, emotional and sexual abuse, and a sense that all that was good and noble in their lives has fled from them.

Two Enemies: The Rebels and Their Own Government

The embittered people of northern Uganda have grave reasons to claim aggrieved status. The soldiers of the UPDF, those specifically charged with the task of protecting all Ugandan civilians, have been so like the enemy in their detestable and vengeful acts that at times it is difficult to distinguish the enemy from the protector.

Ugandan soldiers have engaged in acts of torture and rape of the civilian population they have been ordered to defend. They have engaged in countless summary executions of innocent non-combatants. They have coerced underage Acholi youth into their army only to be further brutalized. They have looted Acholi cattle and done nothing to stop roving cattle thieves from stealing the rest. In fact, Acholi people have lost over three million head of cattle in the last two decades as government soldiers shared in the destruction of the Acholi way of life.

War profiteering is one of the most lamentable aspects of the LRA rebellion. War is hell for all engaged in it—while still remaining extremely profitable for those who prey on the misfortune of others. The Ugandan defense budget has been kept classified for years as a state secret, while army commanders, in particular, have unexplained wealth. When Uganda discovered oil reserves in its western region, it was the army commanders who lined up for a chance to buy up property near the discovery sites.

One lawyer with the Ugandan Human Rights Commission offers her assessment of the legitimate grievances of the Acholi. She relates:

> When UPDF soldiers were disgruntled, they would often take it out on the civilian population. They could easily falsely accuse you of being a rebel collaborator and then try to forcibly coerce a confession from you. False accusations of helping the rebels were a very common form of harassment. The Acholi feel neglected. They cite how no serious development has taken place here in their region of the nation in well over

a quarter century. In the last presidential election the Acholi voted 97 percent against Museveni. Indeed, many in the international community have come to realize that if the government really wanted to end this war, they would have found a way to do so. When rebels in the Allied Democratic Front (ADR) ushered in a rebellion in Western Uganda, they were quickly and decisively squelched.

The native Acholi people of northern Uganda and their neighboring tribes have gradually come to believe that there is a conspiracy against them, since so many people and events have contributed to their subjugation over the last two decades and more.

Notes

1. Todd Salzman, "Catholics and Colonialism: The Church's Failure in Rwanda," *Commonweal*, May 23, 1997, 17.
2. See Robert Antelme, *The Human Race* (Evanston, IL: Marlboro Press, 1992); originally published in French in 1957.

3

The Girls of St. Monica's School

In Search of the Promises the Future Holds

Imagine 250 young girls living together, ranging in age from fourteen to twenty-four years of age, in the heart of the war zone where rebels rule. This is ground zero, the center of Gulu, the largest town in Acholiland, where daily vulnerable young females go missing. They are kidnapped into sex slavery to be placed in the unrestricted service of unscrupulous rebels. St. Monica's is a girl's boarding school where tailoring and catering are the chief subjects taught and safety and security are its prime assets.

The walls surrounding this compound are higher than others in the city, topped with jagged, sharp glass. It is arguably the safest place in Gulu. The Gulu prison is directly across from here with its many armed guards who could quickly be mobilized in support of St. Monica's girls should the school fall into a crisis situation.

This vast compound has only one entrance. It is always attended to by a gateman and, in times of insecurity, a guard. Even the guard and the gateman are not trusted at night with the key to the gate. Once the gate is chained at dusk, they are required to turn in the single key to the gate to the convent. The sisters, vigilant at all times, know full well that even the noblest of men, men of their specific choice, can suddenly fall prey to physical force, bribery, or coercion from those seeking that key—and the tragic victims would be their girls.

No girl from St. Monica's has ever been kidnapped while lodged here at this securest of compounds. Yet some 40 to 50 percent of the entire student population shares a terrible past—they were thrown into the LRA rebellion against their wills. They were abducted from elsewhere, principally from home, and this has become their safe haven after escape or rescue.

The girls at St. Monica have come to believe that they have to struggle and fight for their future—nothing will come easily or just be handed to them. It is obvious that life in the bush has contributed to this assumption in a large measure for many of them.

Most of these girls have not had nurturing parents—some no parents at all. Many of them have become child mothers themselves while still extremely young, teenagers of thirteen or fourteen years of age, or tragically, even younger. The rebel commanders in particular fear HIV/AIDS. They want young girls the most because they are simply presumed to be HIV negative, virgins who might even contribute to their health if they are lucky enough to have sex with them. This horrific false assumption has lead to the violation of prepubescent girls across Acholiland, who are now traumatized for life by sexual violence in the extreme.

These young girls shoulder parental responsibility at an incredibly early age, and this at a time when these teenagers might expect to just play and do the things that other kids their age do everyday. It is painful for me to see the continued cycle of neglect that leaves children without the love and affection they need to embrace life.

St. Monica's is like a protective shield around these young mothers. Like a mother's arms wrapped securely around them, they know that they are in the company of others, women stronger than themselves, who would fight for their well-being and that of their children no matter the danger.

Many of these girls have dropped out of school sometime in the past or lost their childhoods in the crucible of this LRA war. They walk with a sense of regret and past failure. St. Monica's offers these girls, in the most fragile of moments in their lives, protection, stability, and a chance to believe again in the power of goodness over all else.

The Girls of St. Monica's

Meet Victoria Abio and her daughter, Joy

Victoria is eighteen years old and her playful baby is nine months. They are anything but a conventional mother and daughter. For more than seven years, Victoria was thrown into war in northern

St. Monica's School—Victoria and Joy with Sister Rosemary

Uganda, forcibly abducted into the LRA. Guns, hunger, sexual abuse, and unrelenting loneliness—these have been Victoria's companions throughout her formative years. While other kids her age were playing sports and joining the drama club at school, she feared for her life daily. Indeed, her kidnappers often preyed on that fear.

As I sit in the shade with Victoria and her baby outside St. Monica Girls' Tailoring Centre in Gulu they present themselves like any other mother and child. The baby seeks comfort from her mother's breast and afterwards gently drifts off into sleep. Victoria is serene and dignified. She is unabashedly unafraid to tell her story, even with all its raw pain still intruding into her young life. These days she is fighting to spiritually reclaim her life from her rebel captors. They stole her from her family when she was only ten years old. She is only slowly being released from the shackles of a very dark past.

The night of her kidnapping from her village at Pabango is etched in her memory. Victoria reminds me that the LRA invariably come under the cover of darkness to steal children. She recalls how the rebels were grabbing all the children they could get from her village. One family who lived in her vicinity had all seven sons taken that same fateful night that the rebels captured Victoria. Strangely, she was the only girl they succeeded in abducting from her village. The rebels were binding them together with rope in groups of three. All the children were forced to begin immediately a march toward southern Sudan, the LRA stronghold. One of the boys, a friend of Victoria's, refused to march and was knifed in the hand and forced to comply.

The night she lost her childhood, Victoria could not have imagined that she would be with the rebels for more than seven years. They gave her a gun and a place in the frontline of battle. Often she would hear shouted at her: "Kill or be killed." What Victoria did not know when she was abducted is that commanders routinely rape the girls they steal from home and that others are given to younger soldiers as rewards for military victories and sustained service in the LRA. They become the new plaything for the soldiers, starting often as young as twelve or thirteen years old. Victoria soon encountered this evil.

As Victoria finds the courage to speak of the sexual abuse she was forced to endure, she casts her eyes to the ground, avoiding all eye contact. Victoria tells me she was raped twice at age twelve and then given to a commander her father's age as his "wife" at age thirteen. Nearly 90 percent of the girls who manage to escape the clutches of the LRA escape with sexually transmitted diseases, often HIV. If the girls refuse the demands of their captors they are threatened with death.

The children are made to believe there is never a chance of escape. Some are forced to kill a parent or a sibling at the moment of being kidnapped. This creates a trauma deliberately planned to stigmatize these new recruits and to destroy any sense of home and family. Victoria was told that her community back home would punish her with fury for the killings she was forced to participate in while in the bush. She was told that they would punish her slowly and secretly by grinding up glass bottles and placing the broken glass in her food. Within six months she would certainly be dead. Young and impressionable, she at first believed her captors.

Victoria lulled her captors into believing she would never run away. But she had also heard on the radio while in the bush that child soldiers forced into the LRA were not being punished back home. Throughout her captivity she harbored a dream of one day returning home.

Joy was just four days old when mother and daughter escaped. The day before, they had had an exhausting day, moving around quickly all the time. At around 11 PM, Victoria removed Joy from the carrying sack on her back and saw immediately that her baby's face was completely red from rubbing against her back throughout the day. Filled with protective, maternal instincts toward this newborn whose life was in peril and whose future was totally in her hands, she went to the river to fetch water to bathe the baby. The rebel leader who had fathered Joy detected Victoria's concern and also sensed that something might happen soon. He asked, "Victoria, why do you want to go home? They'll kill you there." The commander placed four boys as bodyguards to surround Victoria.

Around 6:00 the next morning, this clever and very self-reliant young woman, carrying her baby in her arms, was able to elude her captors. She raced to the high grass where they both fell silent and completely still. Her baby, exhausted, never whimpered to let the squad in search of them discover their whereabouts. Victoria prayed: "God, if you wish, let me die here with my baby." Rebels kept pacing about in the high grass in pursuit of them. One of them came within ten feet of them, threatening; "I'll kill you now if I find you."

Why did Victoria embrace courage that grace-filled morning to escape her tormentors or die attempting to reach freedom? After all, she had been with them for more than seven years. Why was this precise moment the propitious time to act? Joy.

Baby Joy was all the difference. Victoria could now live for her child, she could claim the resilience that mothers possess in protecting and providing for their own. While she could not find the courage to flee for herself, she could do the seemingly impossible for the offspring God gave her to nourish. I believe her actions show the magnanimity of the human spirit, the great-heartedness that is possible for every person. Kidnapped young mothers in the LRA all want to flee with the children born to them in captivity, despite the fact that they were born of a brutal attack on their person. Victoria is a person gifted with a magnanimous character; she knew that she could expect great things of herself when prompted by love to act on behalf of her child in peril.

Victoria still feared some of the rebel's predictions. Her first three days in freedom she ate nothing that was given to her, fearful someone might have slipped broken glass into her food. Ugandan army soldiers found her on the road and promised to return her home. She ate in their company only after they ate some of the same food in her sight. The rebels were extremely good at destroying trust.

St. Monica Girls' Tailoring Centre, where this remarkable mother and daughter have chosen to continue to live, is staffed by six members of the Sisters of the Congregation of the Sacred Heart of Jesus, who offer them unfailing personal support. The sisters give that same devotion to over 260 young girls, many of whom sadly have a story to tell very similar to Victoria and Joy's. Here the girls befriend one another, learn a skill, and walk into their futures in freedom. Here they hear the sisters' voices raised in song and praise instead of the jeers and insults of the rebel commanders.

Nancy and Her Daughter, Peace

At St. Monica's, there is one girl whose physical appearance, at first sight, frightened me. Her face is distorted in a hideous fashion. Nancy Avoch is a seventeen-year-old survivor of this LRA war who got caught in the crossfire. A frenzied and fierce battle ensued on her last day with the LRA. She was hit with a barrage of bullets striking her arms, thighs, and chest. She fell to the ground and tried to remain hidden, covered by a fallen banana tree. After the battle, rebels were pacing all over the battlefield, searching for survivors. She heard one rebel boy say to another, "If we find any girls alive let us rape them first before finishing them off." She froze at the sound of those words and remained absolutely still; all the while she was bleeding profusely and in excruciating pain.

When the rebels moved on from that place, Nancy got up the nerve to stand and move. She had no idea where she was or where she was going. She was in a trancelike state. She came upon a passion fruit tree and took a piece of fruit off the tree to eat. She couldn't eat or speak. Startlingly, she realized she had no lower jaw. She had also been hit by bullets in the face and remarkably had not realized it to that very moment.

The bullets that struck her face resulted in massive and irreparable distortions in her physical appearance. Nancy was in Lacor Hospital in Gulu for four months of recovery after Ugandan soldiers found her half dead in the bush. At Lacor Hospital, an Italian doctor who took a particular interest in Nancy's condition was able to have her transferred to a hospital in his homeland. Nancy received specialized treatment in Europe for over one year. Disappointingly, the highly skilled medical practitioners there were still unable to rebuild her jaw and lower face in a way that would restore her original features. Nancy still looks as if someone took a large machete and just started slashing her face. People are repulsed by her appearance.

Nancy was abducted from their family home with her sister Agnes. The rebels decided at the last minute not to take Agnes because she was not an attractive girl, one rebel referred to her as the ugly one in the bunch. Nancy was the most physically attractive among the daughters born to her parents—the rebels took her alone. The LRA just abandoned Agnes in a neighbor's hut and left her there.

Nancy relates how the initial march with the rebel group lasted a solid month. At one point, they came to a river, which was flowing very fast, swollen from the rain. The captives were tied with a rope and Nancy nearly drowned. One of the others saved her. Sister Rosemary, the headmistress at St. Monica's, has heard innumerable stories of children from Gulu drowning in the Aswa River, all tied up in ropes and unable to swim. Newly abducted recruits are considered disposable people, their deaths inconsequential. Hundreds have likely died in the rivers after abduction, guilty of not knowing how to swim.

Nancy knows that she lost her physical charm, but not her life or her spirit, to her rebel abductors. What strikes me the most is that what brought Nancy into this war, the fact that the rebels found her face and body shape attractive, was what the rebels themselves destroyed. It is their bullets that made her face hideous, harming also her chest, arms, and legs.

Nancy is forever grateful to God that she was never sexually abused while in the LRA. This is exceptional considering the reason why she was taken. She says she will always be grateful to God for sparing her this pain. Still, an indisputable fact of her young life is that she conceived and bore a daughter she named Peace. When Nancy is asked the identity of the father of her baby, she refuses to disclose it. She tells most people that he is a university student. She says that she has little contact with him now.

Nancy tells her close female friends another story; to them she confides the truth. The father of her baby was a Ugandan soldier. It was a UPDF soldier who took advantage of her vulnerability in her recovery process, having sexual relations with her resulting in her becoming pregnant. That soldier has had absolutely no contact with her since. No university student is romantically interested in this young woman, who has lost so much to this insane war in her homeland.

My heart aches for Nancy. What she has endured strains the moral imagination. No one of us in the human family ought ever to encounter what this young girl encountered. The rebels stole her from her family. These same rebels abandoned all other female abductees that day except Nancy because they were not attractive enough to suit them. In other words, from the outset, this young woman was treated like a commodity, not a person. She was nothing more than a prize that would be given away to a military commander—but not until that commander had proven himself.

While anticipating the day when the rebels would have their victory and Nancy would be given as the prize, the rebels encountered a military defeat. All the while, they remained willing to place Nancy in a situation of extreme jeopardy. She fell victim to horrific violence in that sudden ambush, an ambush that certainly spared her from the future sexual violence that would have been unleashed on her in the days to come if she were forced to remain in the company of the LRA. The military forces of her homeland rescued her. Then one of the rescuers impregnated and abandoned her.

This is the devastating truth about the youth in northern Uganda that has gone largely unreported to the rest of the world. This is why their parents and their grandparents cry themselves to sleep at night. No one, most especially their beloved offspring, has been safe in the homeland for a long time. They are not safe in their homes, not safe in their schools, not safe anywhere. There is guilt in all this insecurity, a guilt that is overwhelming and unavoidable. Parents all across northern Uganda feel guilty for not being able to secure a safe environment for their children.

I find it most intriguing that Nancy has chosen to give the name Peace to her lovely newborn daughter. Her child's face beams with spirit and delight. I am reminded of the fact that we always want for our children and our grandchildren the blessings of life that, for whatever reasons, eluded us in our past.

Two young women at St. Monica's, Victoria and Nancy, both lost their youth and their innocence to the ravages of war. Victoria was impregnated by the rebels, Nancy impregnated by the rescuers. Victoria named her baby Joy, Nancy named her baby Peace. I wonder what strength lies hidden in these child mothers. They embrace in their arms the children born of brutal and exploitative acts by men accustomed to administering pain and affliction to others. These mothers see only peace and joy in their babies.

Women with a Future

Strong and wise African women are demanding a more just and compassionate social order. They have a vision. They have more than a dream about reinventing their communities—they have specific plans, lots of them.

They first want to place the priority on the youngest, their children, with extensive educational reforms. They know that it is their children who are among the least educated anywhere in the world. A staggering 40 percent of African teenagers are not in school. Instead they go to work doing menial tasks, lacking school fees. The future of promise is then cut loose. That is simply unacceptable to them.

These women are not naive. They know that educational reform can only succeed if it is accompanied by other monumental changes—

tackling corruption, empowering the poorest through microfinance plans so that all contribute to the common good, reinvigorating the health care system, electing more political leaders who share their passion. Someone has to think big—surely the problems themselves are big and will demand comprehensive solutions.

Where others see insurmountable blockades and barriers, Sister Rosemary Nyirumbe sees possibilities and promise. Faced with the formidable task of getting northern Uganda back on its feet after two decades of war, it will be people like Sister Rosemary who will make it happen. She is committed to the education of the most vulnerable victims of this war, the girls she serves. Rosemary firmly believes there can be no peaceful future for northern Uganda without the full participation of her girls; indeed, they will lead the way into the promises the future holds.

Throughout 2002, Sister Rosemary appealed directly to the girls who were abducted into the bush. She did this via radio announcements and the response was staggering. Hundreds of girls said yes to Sister Rosemary's invitation. It is known far and wide that this crusader is true to her every promise. Sister Rosemary promised that their babies would have a safe haven at her school. She promised to impart practical skills that will lead to jobs. She promised throughout it all to provide food, shelter, and love for the girls and their children

The girls Sister Rosemary ministers to are among the most stigmatized of all youth. They regularly encounter cruel remarks within their home communities that make them grow more and more bitter: "You are carrying the child of a murderer," "You are damaged goods," "You are a disgrace to your family and to all of us." Sister Rosemary has set her heart on healing the wounds of this war. She is starting by healing the wounded spirits of these child mothers who lost so much of their self-esteem to the nightmarish disaster in their homeland. This determined nun has given hundreds upon hundreds of these girls vocational skills, an income, and taught them the techniques and know-how that will enable them to be self-sufficient in the future. Rosemary says it all so succinctly: "I want their heads up, and the girls moving away from begging."

On her trips abroad, Sister Rosemary always takes with her the beautiful craft work of her girls to show to others and to sell on their behalf. This is one concrete measure that reinforces for the girls that

Classes at St. Monica's School

they can make something valuable that others will want and that will help them generate income. The items that are most popular are necklaces the girls make from discarded paper. It is rolled very, very tightly into beads, which are then dyed multi-colors and strung together. The materials for crafting these necklaces cost practically nothing but the task is labor intensive. The final outcome is a gorgeous piece of jewelry that originates from discarded material. One woman who purchased a necklace while Sister Rosemary was visiting Cleveland, Ohio, relates how, several times a day while wearing that particularly precious necklace, she lets her fingers move gently across the beads. She pauses for a moment. That moment becomes a prayer as she calls to mind the girls who crafted this treasure and she asks God to favor their future with grace and goodness.

Rosemary has a sense of the global church and the call to worldwide solidarity. She knows that in God's family we all belong to one another and are co-responsible for one another's future. For years she has hosted at St. Monica's a group of Italian lay missionaries, members of the Voluntari Missionari Magentino. They have been helping to construct the buildings on this compound since 1982. They are electricians, carpenters, bricklayers, and craftsmen with a wide variety of skills that they want to place at the service of the poor. They once told Rosemary that Italian is the language spoken in heaven. She diligently went to work teaching herself Italian. Today she can easily communicate with her Italian co-workers in their native tongue. While she never really believed Italian is her future in heaven, she did want to honor their contribution to St. Monica's by learning their language.

Her Excellency Yoka Brandt, the Netherlands ambassador to Uganda, paid a visit to St. Monica's to see the good work done here that she had been hearing about. She asked Sister Rosemary to name her current priority. Rosemary took her to the place on the compound where the youngest were being cared for in a makeshift daycare. There were over eighty children in a place built to accommodate a dozen. Many of these infants and toddlers were the children born in the bush to the girls now studying tailoring at St. Monica's. "These are my priority" was Rosemary's simple, direct answer. Within twelve months of that conversation, the Netherlands embassy was able to finance a large new daycare center built for one hundred children.

Sister Rosemary wants St. Monica's to be a blessing for the entire city; thus, her strategic plan includes the establishment of a medical clinic. Already St. Monica's has the best reputation in the region for empowering disenfranchised girls, training them in income-generating skills. Now Rosemary wants to reach out more directly to the entire community. Some of her sisters are trained nurses and could be of valuable service to the residents of Gulu if a clinic could be established. Sister Rosemary would also like to see the girls of St. Monica's who are HIV-positive able to be treated right on the campus instead of having to go out for their medical treatment.

A new dormitory is about to be completed at St. Monica's that will house more than twenty young child mothers with their offspring. This is the first dormitory specifically designed to give the young mothers and their children a sense of greater privacy and as close to a homelike environment as is possible. Rosemary went to northern Italy and to the United States to tell the stories of her girls to Catholic communities who generously contributed the resources for this project to go forward.

Sister Rosemary believes in handing her girls hope on graduation day. Yes, the girls will receive a diploma. They will approach Sister Rosemary and receive a handshake, or more likely a hug, from the one who is more like mother than headmistress. But these girls will also receive a new sewing machine, and a bolt of new material, as well as a confidence born from walking among people who have believed steadfastly in them and in their future. In the end, there is no substitute for this.

In December 2007, the global television network CNN named Sister Rosemary one of their Heroes for Peace. Perhaps because the international community has been forced to face so many tragedies in recent years, the plight of the extremely vulnerable youth of northern Uganda has received scant attention. This has been a forgotten crisis in the human family. Sister Rosemary and her ministry have been highlighted by CNN so that now millions more members of the human family are familiar with the daily struggles of these girls whose chief desire is simply to live in their homeland in peace.

4

Child Soldiers
The Youthful Faces of War

In America's heartland, the Amish people hold an enviable reputation for their love of the simple life and their commitment to a nonviolent lifestyle. In a small town in rural Pennsylvania called Nickel Mines, a dozen Amish children walked to their one room schoolhouse on an early autumn day in 2006, a day like any other school day. They went to study and learn; they went to embrace their future. Before they reached their lunch recess five young girls, aged seven to thirteen, met with violent deaths. They were slain in their classroom by a crazed man unleashing his aggression upon all females by sending bullets flying at these innocent young girls.

The gunman, a thirty-two-year-old truck driver named Charlie Roberts, was bent on killing young girls as a way of achieving revenge for something that happened to him when he was young. When he stormed this Amish schoolhouse he sent all the boys outside. He ordered some of them to help him carry in items needed to tie up the girls. As they complied with his demands, their female teacher and her mother, who by happenstance was visiting the school that day, seized the moment and quickly exited the schoolhouse to call for help. Roberts ordered the boys to stop them, threatening to shoot everyone if their teacher escaped. This time all the male students refused to follow Robert's orders. He immediately backed down and barricaded himself behind the only entrance to the schoolhouse, securing it with two-by-fours. When alone with the girls he tied them up and began shooting them, execution-style at point-blank range.

The entire nation was stunned. How could this happen in one of the most bucolic and peaceful communities in the heartland of

America? How could this happen in one of our schools, a place traditionally synonymous with safety and learning? Innocence was murdered in that small Amish schoolhouse. A confounding, mystifying evil, wickedness beyond our comprehension had struck Americans who were totally unaccustomed to such aggression. Amish children slaughtered in school, a deadly assault against the most vulnerable, turns all our normal expectations upside down. We no longer know what to expect when the world as we knew it seems to spiral out of control.

Violence against children is particularly repugnant to the human spirit. The moral outcry surrounding the deadly shootings at Columbine High School in Colorado in April 1999 remains etched in our collective memory as a nation. Twelve students were slaughtered with one of their teachers before the attackers turned their violence on themselves and committed suicide. Eric Harris and Dylan Klebold could not have taught themselves all that is necessary to engage in the act of waging war. It is far more likely that a "culture of death" had made deep inroads in their lives. This deadly gun violence involving youths made Americans look at themselves in far more critical ways than we were accustomed to. The unavoidable question became: "Who among us, and what forces, influence our young in ways that lead them to kill?"

This is precisely the feeling of our Ugandan sisters and brothers who have suffered unspeakable crimes unleashed by the LRA. They too have known the same kind of confounding, mystifying evil, an evil that has changed the face of their common life in a lasting way. School shootings, which draw instant media attention, are an aberration in the United States. In Uganda, assaults on both primary schools and high schools are an awful but regular occurrence. The rebels target them specifically because schools hold just what these rebels desperately need to replenish their ranks and continue their struggle: defenseless children. They come to schools in search of boys and girls to make war on their future. The rebels know from two decades of experience that they are capable of being coerced into doing terrible deeds or are simply killed for their noncompliance. Children gather daily in great numbers in schools across Acholiland. The school has become the new battleground as children become the new face of war.

War unleashes hell. In this way, all wars are like one another.

What sets this LRA conflict apart from other wars? In this war, children have been brainwashed and then forced to fight and kill. Children have been made direct accomplices in an incongruous mix of religion and brutality. Bloody violence, sexual slavery, and murder scar their childhoods in this guerilla war unlike any other war waged by men.

The Atiak Secondary Technical School is a boarding school for young people, training them to enter various trades. This popular school in northern Uganda attracts hundreds of students who do not see themselves going on to a college but desire instead to enter into one of the trades after completing high school. In its school district, Atiak has an unmatched reputation for preparing young people to enter into one of various trades such as carpentry or mechanics. Atiak School is something unusual in Uganda; it's a location where children can find a future.

Atiak School is Uganda's Columbine, the school setting where death once made a massive entrance, changing everyone's perception of life by its unimaginable horror. Columbine and Atiak are now infamous in their respective countries for the same lamentable reason: being the place where young people died senselessly, where futures were destroyed, not made.

On April 20, 1995, hundreds of men, women, and children were rounded up by the LRA rebels and forced to march outside their village of Atiak to a nearby river. Raiding the dormitories of Atiak School, LRA rebels abducted many of the teenage students into the forced march leaving the village. There they were separated into several groups according to their sex and age. The LRA general Vincent Otti, second in command to Supreme Commander Joseph Kony, chastised them for their alleged collaboration with the government forces trying to stamp out the LRA rebellion.

Then all the men and boys were ordered to lie still on the ground, face down. Three times the LRA commander ordered his soldiers to open fire on this group of approximately three hundred innocent and unarmed boys and men, including the students from Atiak School. The awful fate of the women and children was to watch—to witness the slaying of their sons and their classmates, their husbands, and their neighbors in the village. They were ordered explicitly by the rebels to look straight at the boys and the men. If they failed to do so they too would be fired upon.

It was Vincent Otti himself who gave the order to his troops to shower them with bullets. Not one person got up to attempt to run away, everyone seemed resigned to the fact that their lives would be cut short and ended that day by violence. After the bullets were silent, the LRA rebels were ordered a second time to fire on the dead corpses, followed by the surprising third command to repeat their shooting to confirm their deaths.

One mother who was an eyewitness to this attack told me that she stood by watching and silently weeping for her young son who was among the three hundred boys and men slaughtered that day. Through it all she clung to hope. She refused to be captured by the fear the rebels spread. She remained steadfast in her trust that God would never abandon her. This mother did precisely what was ordered by the commander—she kept her eyes fixed on the rebel's victims, one of whom was her firstborn son. Her gaze was fixed on him; she never looked away even though she feared what she was likely to see. She watched her boy closely with each of the three shootings. It was apparent to her that he was shot, but she believed his wound was superficial. The bullet struck him in the leg. He could survive if he pretended to be dead.

This he failed to do.

The rebels who were searching for any movement among those they had just slain approached him with a bayonet, which they thrust into him with the first sign of movement. The mother, who had been watching him in hope, still could not turn her eyes away from him. Now she watched him and his bloody death in utter despair.

Mothers aren't supposed to be on battlefields; they are not supposed to see their sons being slain. Mothers weren't present on the beaches of Normandy, France, on June 6, 1944, when several thousand soldiers bled to death on the shores of the Atlantic and turned the ocean waters crimson red with their blood. Their hearts and spirits were with their sons, but their eyes never actually saw the deaths.

It is estimated that over sixty students from Atiak School were killed that day, or roughly five times as many students who perished in the Columbine Massacre. Coincidentally, both the Columbine Massacre and the Atiak Massacre happened on the same day, April 20, four years apart. Abductions of youths from their schools in northern Uganda to be thrown into guerilla warfare highlight just how unlike other school shootings in the United States this youth violence is. This war is bizarre in every respect, totally unlike any other. The victims are so young. Perhaps these, the youngest victims, reveal to us a new face of war. Yes, children are the new face of war.

Children are always vulnerable. No matter the age of the one sent into harm's way, every child of God is a son or a daughter, every life is vulnerable, precious, and deserving of safeguards. War slowly takes away all the protections we have placed, like a shield, around those whom we love. It leaves them exposed to this world's evil and its resulting violence in unintended and unimaginable ways.

What happened immediately after the third round of shooting is as bizarre as anything this war has brought. As the women and girls stood immobilized in grief, General Otti spoke to them in a stern voice: "Have you seen what happened here?" his voice betraying someone who was very annoyed and in an agitated state. All who were subjected to this violence and forced to endure it were too numb to answer. A few gathered strength to answer in the affirmative. They simply nodded their heads in silent assent. Nothing more could be asked of them. They remained fearful that no answer at all would only provoke more killings on a day that had already witnessed massive death.

General Otti's voice became louder and louder. In a tense tone of voice he screamed at the eyewitnesses of this massacre. At this scene of unimaginable violence, violence he himself had arranged, he asked of these eyewitnesses: "Now applaud the LRA's work." Those who had been forced to watch the slaughter of their loved ones were now, under threat of death, ordered to applaud the murderers. Reluctantly, they acquiesced to the demands of those who held guns pointed at their heads.

As a priest, people have confided in me the stories of their personal suffering, some of which have been overwhelming. Still, General Otti's cruelty is unlike the brutality I have encountered elsewhere in that it appears to me to be almost inhuman. His actions are so laden with all that harms and destroys humanity that one is left wondering how a human being could participate, let alone order, such commands to be carried out.

Vincent Otti was born in 1946 in the northern district of Gulu, close to the town of Atiak. He carried out this merciless massacre in the place of his birth. This soldier is not a monster who is inhuman. Vincent Otti is not without human origins, not without an identifiable mother and father. Atiak is home, Atiak is where mother and father embraced life and founded a family. Atiak is the place remembered today for its inhumanity.

General Vincent Otti has been charged with thirty-three counts of war crimes violations since July 2002 at the International Criminal Court in The Hague. His actions scream out as crimes against humanity. While his actions clearly violate international law, the attacks he has personally ordered on civilian populations and his enslavement of vulnerable children stand out before the whole world. They propel all of us into a new realm. If we do not actively move against him future generations may rightly hold us all accountable. With the slaughter of innocents comes the unavoidable question: "Did we close our eyes to their peril?"

There exist intrinsically evil acts. Vincent Otti's actions may be the prime exemplar of them in our time. Forced to fight and die in guerilla warfare against their will, the children commanded to do unspeakable acts by Vincent Otti know who stands with them and who abandoned them or looked the other way when they were sent into the war zone.

Before departing from the attack site the rebels selectively rounded up any able-bodied youths to serve as the next generation of combatants and sexual slaves.

"All of us live as if our bodies do not have souls." This is the sentiment expressed by one eyewitness, a woman who had family members killed in the Atiak Massacre. She speaks for all who saw and suffered through the death of loved ones at Atiak. I believe she speaks for all who have endured the terrible afflictions that have always accompanied war over the vast span of centuries. When someone we love dies by war's violence, something inside of us also dies. There is a grave cost to the victim's family, to our global community, and to each of us individually whenever a person dies young, by a violence we failed to stop.

Ironically, it seems Vincent Otti has fallen victim to the LRA's brutality himself. In October 2007, in a time when there was an emerging sense of hope about peace accords being reached between the LRA and the Ugandan government, Joseph Kony and Vincent Otti quarreled with each other. There were reports containing conflicting reasons for their falling out after over twenty years of fighting side by side. It was suggested by the Ugandan government that they were fighting over the US$600,000 that donors had contributed. This financial assistance

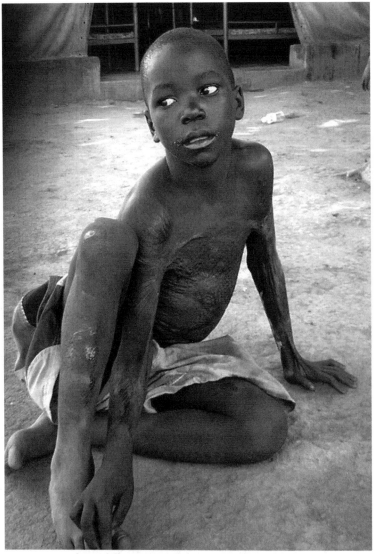

**Ivan, who was badly burned when his
village was raided by the LRA**

was given to the LRA to assist in their preparations for peace talks between the LRA and the Ugandan government to be held in Juba, Sudan. It was also reported that Otti wanted to go forward with the peace talks and Kony did not. What is clear is that a fight between forces loyal to Kony and forces loyal to Otti resulted in a deadly shoot out in which Vincent Otti died. In this unexpected twist, it appears that Vincent Otti fell victim to the man to whom he gave his undying support for many years. The life of guerilla warfare is very cruel.

All across our world, children are falling victim to powerful forces beyond their control—forces that sabotage the bright promise tomorrow should hold for them. The arming of children is among the greatest of these evils. I met scores of young returnees from this guerilla war in East Africa. Pressed into lives of perpetual danger, they find that it takes all their energy just to survive. A common bond shared by all of them is their resiliency; they possess deep reserves of stamina and endurance. I sensed that some stayed alive by sheer willpower. To survive each passing day was their singular goal in life.

As you listen to their true stories, I ask you to attempt to place yourself in their position. Journey vicariously, in your moral imagination, to their exact place in the human family. It is a place where no child should ever have to go, a place too alarming for most adults to be willing to ponder.

A warning. I have attempted to do this and I have repeatedly failed. On the night of May 11, 2003, a large group of seminarians in the Archdiocese of Gulu in northern Uganda were abducted and thrown into guerilla warfare. I know a lot about life in a seminary. I have lived thirty of the last thirty-nine years of my life in a seminary.

I became a seminarian when I was very young, fourteen years old. I remained in the seminary until priestly ordination twelve years later. For the last two decades, I have lived in a seminary, first as a graduate student, later on as a faculty member teaching courses in moral theology. Some of the seminarians abducted were approximately the same age I was when I first entered seminary life. It is a realistic expectation that I could understand just what is entailed in the transition from seminary to a new life outside the seminary.

When that new life includes killings in the LRA, I am completely unable to grasp the situation. When it comes to the forty-one seminarians of Sacred Heart Seminary who went missing after a terrible raid by LRA rebels on their seminary campus, for whom the new life was war, I cannot even begin to imagine the pain. I have tried and failed.

Eight years after the attack at Atiak, the LRA could still move around with impunity and strike at an all-boys school, taking as many young men hostage as they desired. This is a bewildering fact about our world that challenges many of my previous assumptions about how we protect our young from those bent on hurting them.

May 11, 2003—Sacred Heart Seminary under Siege

Meet nineteen-year-old David Lacony, a seminarian of Sacred Heart Seminary in Gulu Archdiocese. The Scriptures tell us that the biblical king David made a striking appearance, a youth handsome to behold. Our Ugandan David bears this king's name and physical resemblance—tall, dark-skinned, and athletic. Yet there is sadness in David Lacony's face that is unmistakable. One wonders what kind of inner wounds he hides.

David felt drawn to be a priest from his earliest years. He was inquisitive about the lifestyle and daily routine of priests he admired. By the time he was fourteen years old, he had applied and been accepted to seminary high school. In his first two years in the formation program his greatest challenge was to prove that he could succeed academically and remain highly motivated. On the night of May 11, 2003, his perspective on his personal challenges would change forever. In the months and years that followed, David would be challenged most to find a way to forgive himself for unspeakable acts he was forced to commit. That night he was abducted from his seminary, along with forty other seminarians, and thrown into the hell that is guerilla warfare.

That Saturday began as a sunny day, the sky above Gulu clear blue. Daily life was proceeding along its normal routine for the seminarians, as normal as life can be in a land that holds so much peril for youth. The Ugandan army had stationed four soldiers as a security detail to guard Sacred Heart Seminary. No one could have predicted the stunning events that were about to unfold at this seminary campus. Only two faculty members remained home that night, Msgr. Sebastian Odong and Father Cyprian Ocen.

A steady stream of night commuters began pouring into the compound just before twilight. Sacred Heart Seminary was considered one of the most secure compounds in Gulu. Children fled there each night for a secure night's sleep. Nearly one hundred of them slept on the large veranda of the administration building. This holy place was their safe haven.

David retired to bed around 10:00 PM. Shortly after midnight, he was abruptly awakened by the sound of gunfire. Shots were ringing out from outside the walls of the seminary buildings. The rebels had surrounded the school under cover of darkness and were attempting to storm the seminary compound. When they failed to enter, they began shouting and demanding that the entrance door be opened.

David's first prayer while encountering this sudden threat was: *"God, show me the way."*

The security detail of four soldiers fled at the sight of the rebels. One climbed a mango tree and remained hidden, the other three fled in haste on foot. The rebels began breaking all the glass windows and then sent a small child through one window to open the entranceway from inside. As the child opened the door, twenty or more rebels raced inside. They were shooting their guns into the air to frighten everyone in the compound into compliance. David and those in his dormitory scurried about; most simply hid under their beds.

In the mayhem, one of the night commuters, a young boy, was shot in the head and killed. Within minutes, the rebels invaded David's dormitory and the seminarians were quickly rounded up and tied together with rope. The rebels searched for valuables and things to steal, which they made the seminarians carry. Now everything was happening very fast. The life David had known—daily Eucharist, common prayers, study, and sports—in an instant, everything this young man cherished was gone.

Not everything.

David remained a man of prayer. His captors could not destroy what was happening inside him. Prayer became the sole constant in his life. When everything else was stripped away from him, this alone remained. He knew that God wasn't about to flee from him, as the security detail had done, when he fell into extreme danger.

The forty-one seminarians, along with a few of the night commuters, were then made to commence a walk that would last the whole night and next day. They marched out of the seminary into a very uncertain and precarious future. Many of the seminarians wondered if they would ever return alive. Still no one cried; weakness was punished swiftly and severely by the LRA and everyone knew it. They marched at a fast pace, barefooted, their feet becoming cut on sharp rocks and bleeding. They never stopped. The next morning a helicopter of the Ugandan army passed overhead. They were ordered to lie still in the brush in order to avoid being detected. They marched all day Sunday until late in the evening. They finally arrived where the commanders and other rebels were waiting. There were more than sixty rebels and another fifty abductees at the makeshift camp, mostly abducted teenagers.

Back in Gulu, word spread quickly that the seminarians had been kidnapped. Parents and family members of all the seminarians flocked to the school to see if their children were among the unfortunate ones missing. Here there were tears and loud crying and wailing. Some parents wanted to mobilize themselves into an army and go into the bush and fight for the return of their children. The religious leaders on the scene could only comfort them in their overwhelming grief and counsel them not to risk causing greater harm to the situation by chasing after this heavily armed brigade that kills with impunity.

The first words the LRA commander spoke to David Lacony and his companions startled him like nothing he had ever before heard: "Have you ever seen anyone killed? What if I kill five of you right now?" The LRA are notorious for preying on the fear of those they capture and brutalize. David tells me the commander's name was Kamdulu Onen, and they feared him the most. He divided the seminarians among other commanders to isolate them from one another and to make them harder to find by those who might seek to rescue them. In David's group there were four seminarians, five other young abductees, and four rebel soldiers. They marched toward southern Sudan the next day for between ten and twelve hours. They had not yet been offered anything to eat while in captivity. Late on Monday night they were given some beans to cook. They boiled some water and cooked the beans, the first food they had eaten in over two days.

David Lacony relates to me two terrible incidents in the coming days that were thrust on them and that were particularly painful for him and his companions.

It began with the initial killing, the first time they were forced to participate in ending another person's life. Some in the rebel brigade had gone to some nearby fields in search of cassava to roast. They encountered two men there farming and immediately abducted them. One commander decided that it was time to have the new recruits fully initiated and started them killing on command. They gathered ten seminarians to witness and participate in this first killing. They were told to get big sticks, which were to be used to strike the men in the head. They were told: "If you fail to kill these two men we will kill you." David became visibly shaken; his fears could be readily seen in his face. As he spoke of this episode, his eyes filled with tears. He relates that he immediately started praying to be spared from this evil. *"Oh God, you are the One who is taking care of me. You know everything. Whatever is to take place now, forgive me Lord for it is not of my own making. I am being forced."* The two men were lying face down on the ground. They remained silent throughout the entire ordeal of being bludgeoned to death.

The first attempted escape and its associated punishment followed. On day ten of their ordeal, two of the seminarians tried to escape in the morning. Rebels raced after them, caught them, and brought them back for punishment. It was decided not to punish just the escapees, but to gather up many of the seminarians for a collective punishment meant to dissuade the others from attempting a similar action. At least fifteen or more seminarians were summoned, forced to remove their shirts and then to lie down on the ground. The rebel brigade began marching over them. Every one of the seminarians thought they were going to be killed. They were preparing for death. The commander said to them: "I am thinking of killing all of you now. No one will care back home." More and more rebels were called to take their turn beating the seminarians. David was severely beaten on the back and buttocks. In the end, they took a machete and cut each of them with two strokes to the back.

It was in the afternoon of the seventeenth day of his captivity when an opportune moment came for David to attempt escape. The Ugandan People's Defense Force attacked David's group in a surprise raid around 2:00 PM. In one flashing instant, David, along with another seminarian named John Paul Rubangakene, decided to run. They ran for dear life, they ran till they could run no more. There is relief sounding in David's voice as he tells me of his final hours in captivity. There is regret as well. He tells me in a sad tone of voice: *"In my heart, I still feel very guilty. I pray for forgiveness."* There is an overwhelming sadness when he speaks of the eleven seminarians that still are held by the rebel brigade.

Throughout his ordeal, David made numerous attempts to protect his soul. I listened to him relate how he yearned to remain joined to God and to the human family while forced to do inhuman actions. When one kills another person, one cuts the ties that bind us to one another in the human family. David realized this truth in a full way.

This young seminarian's unique circumstances drew me to recall Victor Frankl's insight regarding those who have been thrown into utterly brutal circumstances: "Everything can be taken from a man but one thing: the last of the human freedoms—to choose one's attitude in any given set of circumstances, to choose one's own way."[1] The forming of an attitude takes place deep within a person, in the inner recesses of the self. No one can gain access to the self without first being welcomed there. No one truly knows our attitude toward life and what we have experienced unless we confide ourselves to him or her.

Our attitude is directly linked to our inner disposition. It is common among newly recruited youth in the LRA to invent mechanisms to hide their true selves, their innocence, and their refusal to kill. David's inner disposition could not tolerate the idea that he might kill. This action was wholly inconsistent with his entire life's trust. Only if someone directly forced this on him against his will could the performance of such a violent and naturally repulsive action make any sense.

Feeling completely unable to control what was thrust on him, David made a conscious choice to distance himself from his own actions, inasmuch as that is possible for any one of us to do. This is a common trait among the abducted children thrown into war that I have met. They tell me that at the worst, most violent times, they would simply try to step out of themselves to do the unthinkable actions their rebel captors demanded. Extraordinarily, at the same time, David kept possession of that prayerful inner character that kept his spirit alive.

Should he have simply refused to kill and endured his own execution as the consequence of his choice? I have often pondered that most challenging of questions. Who is the victim here, David Lacony or the two innocent farmers he bludgeoned to death in order that he might live? How can anyone answer these questions?

Over time I have come to the conviction that the most accurate description of David in his forced, short life in the LRA is the word *victim*. This judgment is not just my own, I sense it is the judgment also of those two innocent farmers whose deaths occurred by David's hands.

I am deeply curious about the last minutes of life for these two randomly chosen farmers, who deliberately decided to remain still and silent throughout their ordeal. Why were they still and silent if not but in an exercise of freedom, to choose one's own way? I suspect that by David's demeanor they knew whom it was who was striking them. They knew it was a youth, one of their own kinsmen, one who would rather be anywhere else but at this site, doing anything else but hurting them. This might have been their particular way of saying to David, we know that you are not our killer.

I have learned of mothers who were killed by their own boys as LRA rebels were kidnapping them. The rebels demanded it as the condition for their being allowed to live. The rebels especially wanted to start destroying the moral sense and human feelings of their abductees. These mothers, with a simple glance, could gently indicate to their offspring their permission and their forgiveness—dying so their children could live and hopefully one day escape this nightmare. LRA chiefs, demanding all these senseless killings, stand culpable.

In Christian Europe of the Middle Ages, soldiers often did acts of repentance after battle to acknowledge that killing is always a moral defeat that diminishes us all. David's first desire after escape was not to celebrate his release with family and friends but to receive healing through the sacrament of reconciliation. Each seminarian that has been abducted, upon return, has met privately with Archbishop Odama. In these conversations they are encouraged to speak the full truth of their ordeals. It is liberating and excruciatingly painful to admit and name all that they were forced to do in the rebel brigade. The seminarians have been asked by the faculty of their school to place in writing the details of their ordeal, to chronicle their remembrances—even the nightmarish and unspeakable acts they were forced to commit. In this way the full and unvarnished facts of life in the LRA are recorded. Decades from now, others will read these accounts, written so that in the future others may read them and learn something of the nature of evil and turn from it.

The Daring Encounters in Captivity for William Akena

The forty-one abducted seminarians all possessed a close bond to one another and to God. They universally have claimed that it was God and the courage of their classmates that enabled them to live through such hellish experiences and to come out of the war alive and with their faith in God and one another strong.

I was allowed to read the seminarians' accounts of the evil they experienced in the custody of the LRA. What riveted my attention was the manner in which each managed to escape. It seemed that God's providence was discernible in the account of the escape of William Akena. I could see God's saving hand guiding this captured seminarian every moment of the way. Once this teenager was apparently perceived as no longer of use to the rebels they simply left him for dead. Listen to William Akena's own words as he tells us of his final trials in the rebel brigade. William relates:

> Before the officers retired to sleep at night they made sure that all of us were tied up together. They would tie our hands securely to our back in such a way that we sat in a circle. We slept that way in a group of four persons with our heads covered with a large polyethylene bag. Once in this position no one was allowed to go out either to urinate or to relieve themselves. One can only imagine how you would feel urinating on yourself with hands tied. Those who experienced stomach upset had no choice but to relieve themselves right there. I have never seen such inhumane treatment. These things were done to us to make it impossible for us to escape; however they knew we would eventually escape when given the chance.
>
> At long last the rebels untied our hands because we were required to carry very heavy supplies. The rebels had all of us on the move again. We walked the entire day climbing hills, crossing many rivers and valleys that resulted in wounds and

the loss of skin on our legs. Very late in the evening, we were finally ordered to stop the journey for it was getting late. The seminarians were separated into groups from the other captives to do some cooking. After about thirty minutes a message was received indicating that government soldiers were nearby. Immediately, we were instructed to pack up everything and walk quietly, yet swiftly in a scattered fashion so as not to leave behind any signs indicating our direction of travel. We were scared at the thought of getting caught in the crossfire between the government soldiers and the rebels. We walked hurriedly for many hours and at one point I lagged behind, too exhausted to continue. This resulted in verbal insults, brutal beatings and wire whippings, but I could not walk any faster despite the pain they continued to inflict on my head and body. As I became even weaker, my steps faltered and upon falling to the ground they decided to finish me off right there.

A young rebel, about my age, was ordered to stay behind the group and kill me. The rebel became very impatient, making accusations about my walking slowly so the government soldiers would find us and of planning to attack him to take his gun. Finally, I could endure no more and said, "My brother, I am very weak and harmless to you, how can I attack and overpower an armed soldier like you?" He responded to my question angrily by repeatedly kicking and beating me and finally drove the barrel of the gun into my back, all the while shouting that he was a dangerous man who had killed many others more important than me. Mustering some courage, I told him that I could not catch up with the group if he kept on with the beatings. He replied, "Ask your father, am I your father, you idiot?" Exhaustion, thirst and hunger had taken its toll such that I fell to the ground repeatedly. Finally, I told him to do anything he wished, to either release me and let me find my way back home or to kill me, if that is more convenient. He said he would never release me and must leave me for dead. Again, came two heavy blows with the barrel of his gun and he was about to kill me with a stick found behind a bush. His face had changed having a terrifying look with the determination to kill. I quickly requested him to let me say a last prayer to God, for his mercy in accepting my soul to eternal rest. He reluctantly said ok, but to make it quick. Just then, as two more rebels were coming toward us; an older boy and a very young boy, the rebel began the beating again on my head and back causing the loss of vision. I could faintly hear their conversation about smashing my head and exposing the brain. They agreed that I was already as good as dead, so my hands were tied behind my back and the rebel inflicted another final blow. This was the last thing remembered, as I lost consciousness for a long time. The heavy rain drenching my body slowly brought back consciousness in late afternoon of the next day. To be alive was really a miracle, for which I praise and thank God for his deliverance from my executioners.

Remembered

The rebels are fond of telling their captives that no one remembers them back home. Just the opposite is true. The names of the eleven seminarians that remain in captivity five years after abduction are known far and wide throughout all of northern Uganda. Many people pray for them by name daily. Their names are Geoffrey Okello, John Baptist Oceng, Solomon Akaka, Jude Thaddeus Ojok, Patrick Okot, Victorio Omolo, Charles Lwanga Okello, Patrick Rubanakene, Luka Odong, Simon Peter Orwyenya, and Bernard Okot.

Living on Hope

Cosmas and Josephine Oceng, the parents of John Baptist Oceng, live on hope and hope alone. Their son is one of the seminarians still in captivity more than three years after that fateful night the seminary was stormed by rebels. Josephine had a dream that same week, a kind of premonition, that the seminary would be raided. When her daughter Claire told her the morning of the abduction that she had heard at church that LRA rebels had abducted a large number of seminarians she almost fainted at the news that her dream had become cruel reality.

Cosmas and Josephine raced to the seminary immediately upon hearing the news. As they arrived, the names of the seminarians who had been carried off in the night tied up in rope were being read aloud. They didn't have to wait to hear their son's name read, his friend Deogratias approached them with the devastating look that told them without words that the rebels now had John Baptist. It was the day after their son's seventeenth birthday.

The Ocengs invited me to their family home in Gulu. There is a shrine in the main room. Statues of Mary and Joseph encircle the most recent photo of John Baptist. His boyish looks make him appear even younger than he is. There are flowers, prayer cards, and a rosary in front of his photo. His mother tells me she prays for him every morning and evening. I doubt her words. I sense instead that she likely prays for him every hour. She must be wondering all the time where he is and what he is being forced to endure.

Whenever anyone has escaped the LRA, John Baptist's parents seek them out to inquire if they have seen their son. Twice escapees told them that they had seen John Baptist in the company of the supreme commander, Joseph Kony. They believe Kony keeps him close to him as a kind of spiritual advisor. Cosmas tells me: "John Baptist is kept close to Kony. That is why it is so difficult for him to escape. He leads prayers. If he is still alive, that is God's grace. We expect to see him one day."

This trial is overwhelmingly difficult to bear for the whole family. Sometimes Josephine finds herself crying in the middle of the day uncontrollably. Her nine-year-old daughter, Rosemary, tries to comfort her: "Mommy, please don't cry. Mommy, don't think those sad thoughts."

The parents of the seminarians meet every May 11 at the seminary to pray together and to console one another. A massive crowd gathers that day for mass on the seminary campus. Josephine did not attend the most recent May 11 gathering, preferring to keep her long vigil for her son's return private. Cosmas, who himself had been a seminarian for five years when he was young, goes to represent the family.

Immediately after the kidnappings, the seminary was temporarily closed and the remaining seminarians transferred to other seminaries in safer regions of Uganda. A higher, more protective wall was constructed around the entire compound. The seminarians urged the faculty to allow them to return to be closer to their families and to live within their own diocese—even in a time of danger. The seminary has reopened and is filled nearly to capacity.

Josephine tells me she harbors great resentment toward her government for sending only four ill-equipped and poorly trained soldiers to guard the student body, a prime target for the LRA's thirst for new, forced recruits. She also resents the fact that her homeland has for so long a time been neglected by the rest of the world. She relates: "It has taken too long for the outside world to learn of our pains. The Congo has wealth, Sudan has oil, but here in northern Uganda we have nothing valuable so we remain forgotten by others. Ours is the most forgotten crisis in the world."

As Josephine laments the noninvolvement of the international community with this crisis that has rocked her family, I am struck by the validity of her words. I am certain she is right. I review in my mind other regions of the world embroiled in intractable violence in recent times that did receive the involvement of the international community: Bosnia, Kosovo, Sierra Leone, Angola, Congo, and Sudan. Each of them had either valuable natural resources or was strategically located near to powerful neighbors who felt they could not look the other way. In Sierra Leone there are diamonds, in Congo there is coltan, in Angola and Sudan are rich oil reserves, and Bosnia and Kosovo are located too close to the heart of Europe to be ignored. This conflict has been played out in a region of our world that is without commercial, economic, or geostrategic interests. Northern Uganda's greatest asset has always been its people, more than half the population now being children. Uganda has one of the highest birth rates of any place on earth at any time in human history. Its population will likely more than double in our lifetime. Uganda is abundantly rich in children. How could the rest of the world find a way to look away from them?

The names of the seminarians still in captivity have been placed alongside the relics of the Ugandan martyrs in St. Joseph Cathedral in the heart of the city of Gulu. They are the long-suffering victims of this unabated violence; they have known intimately the same horror as the Ugandan Martyrs did 130 years before them. In every era of human history those in power seeking their own ruthless purposes have slaughtered innocent young people.

At the end of every year, on each December 28, Catholics mark the feast of the Holy Innocents. We recall the weeping of mothers and fathers who lost their infant sons to King Herod's fury and fear in a time long ago. That weeping continues on in our day in homes all across northern Uganda in families who do not know if their missing children are dead or alive.

Josephine and Cosmas tell me they would have succumbed to despair long ago if not for the consolation and personal support coming to them daily from their community. Josephine gave me her son's school identity card to place in my prayer book as a daily reminder to storm heaven on his behalf. The card is blood red, the color of danger. His photo is on the inside. Gazing at his face, it appears that he is as innocent as he is young.

The Oceng family has plans for that great day when John Baptist will be freed from this danger. They will celebrate a Mass to praise God for walking them through this storm safely. They also hope their son might have a change of environment. They want him to attend a seminary in the United States or Europe.

Notes

1. Victor Frankl, *Man's Search for Meaning* (New York: Simon & Schuster, 1984), 86.

5

The Loss of Parental Love
The Irreplaceable Treasure

There was a young mother who was particularly close to her four-year-old daughter, Jackie. Jackie would sit on her mom's lap as children's stories were read to her. With much delight this young girl would relish those times, wishing the story hour would never end.

The busy mother had many other commitments that she had to fulfill. That is why she decided that for Christmas she would give Jackie a tape recorder with recordings of her mom reading all of her daughter's favorite stories. This was one Christmas gift, however, that was never used, not even once. When asked why, the little girl responded: "The tape recorder doesn't have a lap."

That child instinctively wanted to be near her mom, close to the warmth and the gentleness that radiated from her. The stories only served as the occasion that brought them together. The heart of the experience was not what was spoken in stories, but what was communicated in far more subtle ways. As that young girl was held and prized by her mother, she came to know an exchange of love. It is that exchange, at times mysterious and transcendent, that feeds the souls of young and old alike. When love is near, God is near. And only love and only God possess the powerful ability to school us in the deeper lessons of life.

What have I learned from observing up close the young and fragile lives of the orphans of this LRA war? Simply put, there is nothing more nurturing than the love of parents and family, and conversely, nothing more painful than its absence from our lives.

Shortly before Christmas in 1988 people around the world were horrified to learn of the explosion of Pan Am Flight 103, a plane bound for America from London. Suddenly, without warning, hundreds of holiday travelers were hurled to eternity on a Scottish hillside. Families eager with anticipation for long-awaited reunions stood in stunned silence as the news of the catastrophe reached them. The longing to be together, to share stories, to gather with family around a table, was transformed in an instant into agonizing grief. Pan Am Flight 103 altered the lives of many families and for a moment it seemed as if the whole world was caught up in the great pain of unexpected violence.

The longing to be home, well captured in the holiday travelers eagerly winging their way, is not restricted to certain seasons of the year. Indeed, the longing to come home is universal and at the core of all human experience. Each of us carries within us the longing for home as a place of safety, security, comfort, warmth, and love. Home is where we can be free, take risks, feel accepted, share who we are, and receive that gift from others.

Home is so central to the human experience that it is the very basis of Jesus' message to us: "Make your home in me as I make mine with you." The wonder of union with the Lord is that it is like coming home. In fact, it is being at home.

As I listen to the stories of those orphaned by the LRA war, I continually touch the pain of children who have lost home, that is to say, have lost everything they hold dear. Some are too young to fully comprehend the enormity and the permanence of the loss. Still, every child's unfulfilled yearnings to be loved wound all of humanity.

Stories of Pain I Have Heard from Children in the War Zone

Oscar is eighteen years old. He is gentle, handsome, and good-natured, bearing no outward sign of the trauma or the excruciating pain that has settled deep in his soul in recent years. He smiles readily. Of all the child soldiers I have encountered, his story is without parallel. No one I have met in my life had been kidnapped six times like Oscar has been and lived to tell the tale. In the course of less than four years the LRA rebels have recaptured him no less than five times after initially stealing him from his family in their village of Lokodi, just north of Gulu.

Oscar's first abduction took place on a Sunday morning as he and four other friends were returning from church after attending Sunday Mass. His dominant memory of that first day was the initial beatings he endured in the bush. He was beaten fifty times with a *panga* (knife). It was just a little foretaste of the life he was about to embark upon against his will. He was twelve years old at the time. The blows he endured can still be felt whenever he lets his mind wander back to that first day of many horrible days in the custody of the LRA.

He was immediately trained in the use of weapons. He vividly recalls that the other rebels were anxious to anoint his body very soon after his abduction. He can remember them taking turns making the sign of the cross on his forehead, chest, and back with oil. It all seemed so strange to him, yet all so familiar. He had been raised as a devout Catholic; the sign of the cross was the first image he learned as a very young child. It was the most familiar image to him. It is one of the more universally recognized images for the entire human family. It is the image the rebels used to try to convince him of the sanctity of their cause.

This first of many captivities lasted only fifteen days. He was sent on expedition, forced to capture other children to serve in the LRA. He made a conscious decision at that moment to risk everything. He simply ran as soon as the first possibility presented itself to him. He knew that this could result in death but he was willing to pay that price. He was only twelve, but he knew what was worth living for and what was worth dying for. The government troops were watching and waiting for them to attack. When they did, chaos erupted. Amid all the chaos, Oscar chose to run. Oscar took the risk. As soon as he was alone, the first act he performed of his own free volition was to immediately throw his gun away.

He ran in search of family and home. Miraculously, he reached them. This time, he did not run right back into the arms of another LRA brigade. But in the future, this would be his fate over and over again. Luckily the same brigade of rebels never recaptured him; in that case death was the routine punishment for deserters like Oscar.

The homecoming celebration was short-lived for Oscar and his close-knit family. Within two weeks of his return nine rebels surprised him and his entire family as they were working together in the fields. Oscar was the only one taken. He was just exactly what the rebels were

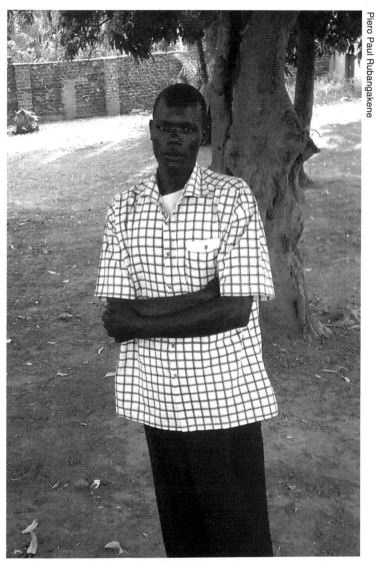

Oscar

in search of: a boy physically strong but still not yet independent and mature enough to counter the rebels' manipulation. The LRA told his family that they were taking him to be educated. He knew that wasn't true.

This second kidnapping lasted much longer, approximately six months. Again he was trained in the use of weapons; again his whole body was anointed with oil. He never gave any indication that he had already experienced all of this.

During this time he was ordered to participate in the looting of many stores and homes across the northern region of Acholiland. They were moving in the direction of southern Sudan when Oscar's rebel brigade ran into a government ambush. There was heavy fire coming from both sides on the ground as well as helicopter fire from UPDF soldiers in the air. In the heat of this battle, Oscar's commander took his gun away from him shouting at him, saying that he was not skilled enough to use it. Oscar never wanted to become skilled in the task of killing. In the ensuing confusion, Oscar ran away and succeeded at escaping once again. On the way home, he was kidnapped by another group of LRA soldiers.

His third captivity was for yet a more protracted period than the first two abductions; he was forced to remain this time with the rebels for over nine months. His brigade was ordered to march to southern Sudan. While in Sudan, he underwent an extensive training in the use of weapons. Oscar would throw away every weapon given to him when he was alone. When the rebels were watching, he treated his gun as his best friend. In fact, he was told that his gun was his mother, his best friend, his everything. He did not believe it but he gave the rebels who captured him every indication that he did.

After his weapons training, Oscar was made to go on military expeditions, raids into northern Uganda to abduct civilians. He was given a weekly quota of seven civilians he was required to kidnap. Whenever he fell short of his captor's expectations he was severely beaten. He tells me he often fell short of his quota and was mercilessly beaten to the extent that he still feels ongoing pain from the punishments inflicted on him. These punishments were not only meted out to him but also to the other young and new recruits. Oscar relates that the older ones were not beaten as much as the younger captives because the younger ones were still being formed. Brutality was seen as the formative experience.

How did he escape this third time? As in earlier escapes, there was a sudden outbreak of fighting between the government forces and the rebels. During this skirmish, Oscar was shot in both legs. He fell to the ground, landing between two dead people. He was bleeding heavily and sensing that this was the final episode in his life—this is the spot where he will be found dead. The other rebels also judged that he was likely unable to survive his wounds, so they took his gun and the bag he was carrying. His rebel brothers left him for dead.

When everything was quiet and Oscar again sensed he was alone, he got up and started to follow the government soldiers' tracks. Oscar knew that he was walking in the direction of home. He did not approach the Ugandan military personnel, still fearful of the kind of reception he might receive. He struggled to reach his home, leaving his blood on the path he trod to reach mother and father. It was his mother who saw him first and there was no question in Oscar of what kind of reception he would receive. The joy of that reunion was the joy of his life!

This young boy remained home and safe for an entire year. While this terrible war waged all around them, Oscar's family remained intact. After a year, at mid-afternoon on a day like every other day, the LRA arrived. They staged a major attack upon the village where Oscar lived. It was around 2:00 PM. When the rebels arrived on the scene, they were anxious to replenish their ranks with new abductees. They first ate a meal in the company of just a few of the villagers and then the rebels rounded up everyone in the village so they could decide for themselves who might serve their purposes. The LRA selected eleven boys and tied them up and led them off into perils few adults would be equipped to endure. Two of the weaker boys could not sustain the rigors of long distance marches. They were ordered to be killed; one was clubbed to death, the other cut. The surviving nine boys were made to stand and watch so they knew precisely what would happen to them if they did not try to remain strong.

This fourth captivity was the longest and hardest to endure for Oscar. It lasted two whole years. His two dominant memories of this time are very telling. First, he relates that what pained him the most was being out of school. He knew that all his friends back home were building their futures and he was in the company of ruthless people wasting his youth away doing what he found abhorrent. Second, he became a sad person, sad at the sight of all these killings. It was all together too much for him. He still does not know how he survived it all. When a large-scale fight broke out with over two hundred rebels fighting against a contingent of UPDF soldiers, he and five others seized the moment and ran for dear life, eventually reaching safety.

Oscar stayed at home six months before the next abduction. The final two kidnappings were for much shorter periods of time.

The last time the rebels stole him from his family they took his older brother as well. One night, Oscar and his brother were out with two LRA rebels on patrol, ordered to kidnap others. When the soldiers fell asleep, Oscar's brother took him by the hand and they ran into the night and eventually into safety.

The brother who helped Oscar escape for the last time, along with his mother and father, were all slain in one of the most horrific attacks the LRA have ever waged. Their village of Lokodi was stormed the night of May 20, 2004, by LRA rebels brandishing clubs and machetes. More than forty villagers were hacked to death in an unimaginable scene of death. Irony abounds. Just as Oscar was finally freed from the clutches of the LRA, these same rebels suddenly turned their violence on his family and killed everyone he loved.

Oscar feels sad when he remembers his mother, father, and brother, who loved him and tried and failed to shield him from the horrors of this war. He now must live with his uncle who mistreats him. He wants to be a catechist; he wants to pass on faith to the next generation. Oscar is very bright, gifted intellectually and with a social maturity that would make him well suited for many professions. When asked why he holds this career aspiration, he answers, "When I came back from the war and my family was massacred, the catechist in our village was the only one who cared for me and gave me words of comfort and hope."

There is a large, stone monument in Lokodi upon which is placed the names of all those who were slain there by LRA rebels. I went there with friends to pray and to remember. I see the names of Oscar's mother, father, and brother etched in the white stone. I feel connected to this tragedy. Oscar has given it a human face.

Concerns for the Future of the Young Victims

On my African sojourns, I have lived among a people who bear some of the most crushing burdens in the human family: the preventable deaths of young and old alike from violence, disease, hunger, and abject poverty, and the pain of living without the sense of a peaceful future. Amidst all these intractable foes there is a terrible temptation to place blame solely on others. It must all be the fault of the rebels, the government, the international community for its noninvolvement, the greed of those who fail to share food and medicine, and so on.

Some people look to themselves instead of blaming others for a world gone horribly wrong. Archbishop John Baptist Odama, the Roman Catholic bishop of Gulu, is such a person. When he meets with the children he will at times kneel before them and ask for their forgiveness. He says: "Forgive me; I should have done more to build you a safer and more peaceful world." The children are shocked to see their shepherd on his knees before them.

On one occasion, while preaching at a large Confirmation Mass at Awach, a sprawling camp for thousands of people displaced by this war, Archbishop Odama asked all the children to stand. "Little ones, you stand up!" There were many adults present, even high-ranking military personnel, who were very curious about this unexpected turn of events. In his fatherly tone of voice he spoke directly to the youth and to them alone: "The condition in which you are growing up is wrong. You lack food, you are dressed poorly, and some of you are very sickly. You have missed your future because you are missing education. You walk in fear. I am sure when you grow up you will ask, 'Why did this happen? Where were our elders to help us and protect us?' I say to you: 'I apologize. I could have done more for you to improve your situation. Forgive me.'" Then he knelt before them.

I imagine the children received a glimpse of what the disciples felt at the Last Supper when Jesus, their teacher and master, knelt before each of them in order to wash their feet. Peace is built from such humble acts of solidarity and love.

On a pleasant July evening in 2007, Archbishop John Baptist Odama invites me to have supper with him at his residence. It has been a year since the cessation of hostilities in the LRA war, and peace talks

Piero Paul Rubangakene

Archbishop Odama and the children

are still ongoing in the southern Sudanese city of Juba. He has been invited to be a part of these proceedings. We speak of what his diocese and his homeland might look like if peace is at long last established across Acholiland.

Archbishop Odama holds many grave concerns for the future of his flock. He confides in me that his greatest apprehension is for the youths abducted into the LRA who are forced to kill close relatives. The potential for long-lasting trauma is so immense, and the number of those youths forced to kill a parent or a sibling so vast, it weighs heavy on his spirit. It has been estimated that close to 10 percent of all abductees into the LRA have experienced killing someone they knew and loved, usually at the moment of abduction.

A child's natural instincts are to yearn endlessly to be held and caressed by parents. The evil this war has brought has utterly destroyed that possibility for far too many children. The absence of those whom they love, dying at their own hands, makes the road to their future an utterly precarious journey, fraught with endless pitfalls too often ending in a place of despair.

Martin is one of the innumerable Acholi youths whose future Archbishop Odama worries the most about. Martin is a thirteen-year-old boy, who was forced one day to watch an execution that would end his life as he knew it. This sort of slaying always bears the potential of utterly severing a young life from the loving and stable roots that nurtured in the past. And that is exactly what the rebels want, that is precisely what they were hoping for from their newest victims.

Throughout this ordeal the LRA assured Martin that this execution would be to his benefit. This first of many killings, he was repeatedly assured, would help him begin the long journey that would harden him to the sight of blood. If he wanted to become a better soldier it would likely be because of this, seeing the blood of his own family members being spilled on the ground.

I have five brothers whom I love very much. As I listened to Martin's story I could not refrain from thinking of my own brothers and my unspoken commitments to them. I spontaneously imagined that Martin felt exactly the same toward his brothers as I have always felt toward mine. That made it all the more troubling for me to hear his words. Martin tells us: "Early on when my brothers and I were captured, the LRA explained to us that all five brothers couldn't serve in the LRA because we would not perform well. So they tied up my two brothers and invited us to watch. Then they beat them with sticks until the two of them died. They told us it would give us strength to fight. My youngest brother was nine years old."

The rebels wanted Martin to sever the ties that bonded him to his family, to commitments to his community back home, to his former identity. The LRA would systematically and methodically try to banish from Martin's consciousness all that lingered from his former self. How else could he be changed from being a child with a natural inclination toward tenderness into an efficient, unfeeling killing machine? The intense trauma of involvement in the killings of family members, close friends, and neighbors is unlike any other trauma. These youths feel that they have lost themselves irreparably when such a tragic event is forced on them.

Children thrust into guerilla warfare lose not only their innocence but also their identity and individuality. The identity of an individual human being makes sense only in the context of relationships with others. What new relationships are they bound to now? Their new companions become the brothers with whom they kill. That says it all.

These children do not want to kill; it is against every one of their natural instincts. In order to make it possible, that which is most distinctively human within them must be crushed, totally suppressed. Empathetic feelings, especially all those emotions leading to compassion and tenderness that are so characteristic of being human and that mark all our lives, especially the lives of children, must be destroyed. Whenever the suffering of others reaches us in a personal way we cannot banish it from our lives, not if we are human.

I cannot even begin to imagine how destructive it must be to a person's sense of identity to be urged to be completely unfeeling and indifferent toward the plight of others. Children are raw humanity. They are not born with virtue—only with the capacity to become virtuous. Impressionable children take their cues from the adults around them. When all the adults surrounding you are brutalizing you and demanding that you too brutalize, something vital to your humanity can die inside of you. One of my students, who viewed all my photos of child soldiers as well as documentaries about the plight of these children forced to kill, approached me after class this morning. She told

A young girl at a camp for internally displaced persons

me she had never before seen such dead eyes as the ones she beheld in these children. Her words struck a deep chord in me.

Dealing with a Past That Will Not Go Away

Richard Opio is one of those young people whose eyes seem so vacant, almost dead. He was abducted at the age that the LRA soldiers most desire in their new recruits. He was thirteen years old, on the verge of adolescence, still young enough and scared enough to be pliable but growing quickly into the physical prowess of manhood.

At his home, from where he was abducted, the rebels forced him to tie each of his parents to a tree and beat them to death. The command on the lips of the rebels was the familiar order: "Kill them now or we will kill them ourselves and then finish you off." His father stood motionless and speechless. The mother told her son in a deliberate and reassuring tone of voice to do what he had been ordered to save his life. He listened to his mother and obeyed her.

The LRA was able to hold on to Richard for two years. He pretended he belonged to them. He did everything he was ordered to. Opio participated in many, many killings. All the time he was constantly on the lookout for that propitious moment when he could escape this insanity.

GUSCO camp became his first home after escape. Richard was able to stay in this nurturing environment for two months. At GUSCO, Richard was encouraged to tell his story, the whole story, to the counselors trained to help him deal with war trauma. He would have been glad to stay there indefinitely. Such an ideal environment for healing is difficult to replicate, especially in this region of the world where resources are so scarce. Richard was released to his aunt who lived in an overcrowded Internally Displaced Persons camp near to their home. His three younger siblings had gone to her after their parents' death. Together with his cousins and siblings, the children all lived in one room.

To my utter amazement, I learn that Richard Opio has not received any counseling since the day he left GUSCO. The sheer numbers of formerly abducted youths in Acholiland are so staggering that local and international agencies trying to respond have been overwhelmed through it all.

Richard has tried repeatedly to talk to his aunt about the killings he was forced to do while in the bush. She always stops him. She has found numerous ways to express that she does not want to hear about his life with the rebels and what he was forced to do. It frightens her. She does, however, seek to assuage Richard's psychological wounds. She tells him: "Do not think about what you have done. You should not worry about it. It wasn't your fault." Her advice, as well intentioned as it is, does not stop the nightmares from coming.

Since leaving the LRA brigade at age fifteen, Richard has been plagued with recurring nightmares. He sees himself cutting off the arms and legs of other children. The screams of his victims are vivid. The shouts of the rebel leaders "Hit him! Hit him!" are as real as if they were happening again. Richard has been forced to find his own solution to the plague of nightmares. If he wakes in the middle of a terrible dream, he lies awake in his bed and prays that the sunrise comes early, completely refusing sleep because of the dangers it holds for him. I call to mind the words of the psalmist "Joy comes in the morning" (Ps. 30:5). Richard Opio is a living icon of this truth.

Laying the Lost Children of War to Rest

In the summer of 2007, I went with some staff members of Caritas International into the fields of northern Uganda to help in healing projects they were undertaking. In the back of our Jeep I noticed they had tied up a young sheep and a small goat. That immediately piqued my curiosity and I suspected we were taking some gifts to nearby villages, including these animals. The Jeep was also stocked with seeds for the next planting.

The adventure that unfolded that day was not at all what I had anticipated.

We were on our way to bury the bones of children of this war who have been slain and have remained lying in the bush, undetected, for several years. The bones were all that were left of their bodies. The sheep and goat were to be slaughtered to help appease the spirits that the local villagers believed were haunting them. Ever since they found the remains of the dead child soldiers the locals were in an agitated uproar. Culturally, it is widely held that the spirits of those who died violently or without respect, whose bodies remain without burial, will not rest peacefully—nor will they let others be at peace.

The village of Palaro Medde is in a rather remote site not far from the Ugandan–Sudanese border. This region had been an LRA stronghold for several years. The villagers tell me that over the course of several months their hunters had discovered ten bodies lying in three separate places in the bush. So fearful and perturbed were some of the locals that they left that place permanently in search of a new home.

The bones were obviously those of young humans, certainly no more than twenty years of age. While all that remained of their bodies were small bones, in each case their plastic footwear and some articles of clothing were also found. It was obvious to the villagers that wild animals had discovered these bodies first. Unburied bodies, they believed, could cause great turmoil for everyone living in the vicinity since their spirits would roam about seeking retribution. Acholi people are highly superstitious and prone to fears about the dead haunting the living.

As soon as we arrived the elders offered words of welcome, and since it looked as if a storm was approaching, they quickly slaughtered the animals and took the entrails with them to spread on the burial sites. I listened to one elder speak directly to the animal he was about to sacrifice. He said: "In ancient times the people of the Old Testament slaughtered animals to sprinkle their blood in acts of purification. I will now kill you for this precise purpose, to cleanse our community of evil spirits."

The community then divided into three groups, since the remains found were still in their three different locations. I walked with about twenty men to the remotest of the sites. One gray-haired elder spoke directly to the dead at the exact moment that we were laying the ground over them. He said: "We did not kill you." He repeats his declaration emphatically: "We did not kill you." He continued: "You are one of us. We love you. We bury you now so your spirit can rest in peace."

It was a long walk back to the village and there was no path to take—we just pushed forward through dense bush. As we were hiking back, my mind was not on the children we had just buried. My thoughts were all fixed upon the children who will survive this bizarre war. I was thinking of Richard Opio, the brothers James and Lawrence, and so many others who were forced to do the unimaginable—atrocities and murders of their own family members in the name of the Lord.

How will they reclaim their humanity? How will they get back their childhoods?

Saints and Martyrs

Every June 3, approximately one million people in East Africa flock to the Ugandan Martyrs Shrine at Namugongo, located just outside Uganda's capital city, Kampala. Some walk on pilgrimage for weeks to reach this holy spot. Yearly a large number of Christians from Nairobi, Kenya, walk for a month praying and singing on their way here. June 3 is the feast day of St. Charles Lwanga and his companions who were put to death on this site in 1886. Pope Paul VI canonized these saints in 1964 and traveled to this famous shrine in 1969 to personally honor their legacy and witness of love.

Owing to religious hatred, King Mwanga killed many faithful Christians in Uganda during the years 1885-1887. Some of them had enjoyed the good graces of the king at his court, and some were even related to him. The youngest of them was St. Kizito, a thirteen-year-old boy who stood loyal to his faith despite the threat of execution. Sadly, far too many young lives continue to end suddenly and violently in this region of the world in the twenty-first century.

On the Ugandan Martyrs feast day on Saturday, June 3, 2006, twelve-year-old William Opio, with his mother and young sister, was farming their land near Gulu, in northern Uganda. Rebels in the LRA abducted all three of them. Within three days mother and daughter were released, but Willie Opio was forced to become a child soldier in this rebel brigade. He may be one of the last victims of a protracted crisis that has become martyrdom for the youth here. Soon after his kidnapping, the LRA rebels and Ugandan government signed a cessation of hostilities agreement as a first step toward a lasting peace.

I met with Opio's mother just days after his abduction. His mother told me that she pleaded in tears for her son's life but the rebel leader told her: "Leave him now with us or we will kill all of you on the spot."

Letting Pain Speak in Poetry

One of the most captivating teenagers I have ever met in my life is Evelyn Lacaa. She is spirited, fun-loving, and wise beyond her years. Popular with her classmates, she was appointed as Head Girl in her school. This is a designation that commands the respect of the students and the faculty alike. Her leadership skills are visible. At a student assembly I witnessed that seemed lackluster, the principal decided to place Evelyn in charge and immediately she had several hundred youth singing out in joy. This has not always been Evelyn's experience; indeed, just the opposite is true.

While never having been kidnapped by the rebels, Evelyn's youthful happiness and embrace of life suffered a double blow as both her parents were murdered by the rebels. At first, Evelyn felt absolutely defeated. The deaths of her parents took away her own will to live. I met her shortly after the death of her mother. Around this time she was asked by one of her teachers to try to give expression to her pain in poetry. The poem "Rebels Have No Mercy" was the first in a series of poems she would write. She was then fifteen years old.

Rebels Have No Mercy

Rebels have no mercy.
In the first year you killed my father.
In the second year you killed my mother.
When I see my fellows moving with their parents,
I think of my once lovely parents.
But where are they now?
Oh! They have been killed by you,
Leaving me in tears from sunrise to sunset,
But rebels have no mercy.

My thoughts wander,
From past to present, from present to past.
When I think of this war in Northern Uganda
I think of nothing else but orphans
And to be an orphan is nothing else but begging
    people's money, money.

Shelter, shelter. The soil is my bed.
No clothes to wear, no money for education.
Yet education is the key to success.
Oh rebels have no mercy.

No food to eat, the dust bin is my hotel.
Rotten things are my favorite,
Diluted water is my drink.
When I beg people don't give to me,
But when I steal, they beat me.
Oh my life is miserable,
Parental love is a dream to me,
But the rebels have no mercy.

Day and night religious leaders are moving,
Pacing about, searching for the solution.
Wake up you too and fight for peace in our land.

You will be glad to know that today Evelyn Lacaa is in possession of a very strong spirit. She is also near to the top of her class academically and has told me she wants to be both a medical doctor and a Comboni sister. She wants to be a healer of bodies and spirits. I am continually astounded at the buoyancy of the youth who have suffered such enormous losses at the hands of the LRA. Evelyn is the embodiment of resilience for all to see. Whenever I am caught up in negative thinking or faced with a challenge too difficult for me to endure, I think of Evelyn and her determined spirit, which would not let the LRA rebels rob her of the life God wants her to live, despite everything that war has thrown at her.

6

Chronicles from the War Zone

What makes this LRA war in northern Uganda so deadly is not the fact that these guerrilla fighters kill with guns and machetes. Far greater numbers of innocent civilians have died from the landmines they hide and the hopelessness they breed. The innocent fall victim here to the hunger war causes, the AIDS it spreads, the malaria and diarrhea that stalk this war zone in frightening proportions, and the over-all devastation ensuing from this conflict that is literally tearing lives apart.

War is indiscriminate; it strikes everyone in its path. In East Africa, war is fought on the home front. The civilian women and children in the path of war bleed just like the soldiers. They all too often are the first to fall victim to the chaos war inevitably creates.

We Gather to Listen and to Learn

On a hot and arid day, our hosts in Gulu assemble together an array of people who each have a very compelling story to tell. It is the morning of July 5, 2007, and today our hosts have brought together fourteen men and women who had experienced the pain of this war in a most personal way. Each of these victims suffered mutilation at the hands of LRA rebels, having their feet, ears, hands, or, in one lovely woman's case, her lips cut off. Now she smiles with her eyes, as if to say to the rebels that the loss of her lips will not hinder her humanity. Many of those who had one or both legs severed from their bodies were victims of the many landmines hidden across this land. The rebels strategically placed these treacherous bombs on paths they expected the civilian population to travel. Each of these victims narrated their story to us as we sought to listen empathetically to tales laden with a crushing sorrow.

Those who had experienced having a hand or arm cut off by the rebels knew that their assailants had two ways of inflicting this irreversible loss: a swift, more merciful way and another way seen whenever the rebels' anger was enraged. If they were in a merciful mood, they would place the limb on a firm surface such as a rock or tree. Then a single fast chop completes the action. If they were inclined to make the suffering last longer, they would place the limb on soft grass necessitating multiple blows and a protracted severing process with its piercing pain.

What struck me the most from their stories was the sense of abandonment most of them would come to experience. All six of the women, and half of the men, told me that, after the soldier's machetes had mutilated their bodies, their spouses eventually left them. Life just grew too bitter from then on. For these victims of war's horror, the loss of a limb meant multiple losses soon to come. The loss of the job that brought security to the family, the loss of a sense of bodily wholeness, the loss of the confident self-image that helped them believe that they could make their future more promising than the past.

The most personal and most painful of all the losses came when the people they loved the most decided to sever ties with them, because life with them now was more burden than anything else.

The most intriguing victim in our assembled group was a woman who looked as if she were in her late teens, but in fact she was the mother of six children. As she introduced herself to the group she told us in a soft voice that her name was Rose. She had a very attractive face that radiated freshness despite everything she had endured. Her left hand had been severed from her body after a small band of roaming LRA bandits had captured her and others in her village.

The rebels had not come in search of her; no, they came to kill her husband, who was a local community leader. Her husband was not at home when the rebels raided the village. Indeed, the rebels mistakenly killed Rose's brother-in-law, believing he was her husband. She had been forced to stand and watch as these rebel soldiers beat her husband's brother to death. Afterward, she was forced to engage in sexual relations with her dead brother-in-law as the rebels stood back and gawked. The rebels are always searching for some new way to exert their power, to display their dominance, to prove that with their authority they can force anyone to do anything at any time at their command.

As I see Rose deliberately, albeit tentatively, taking steps to touch the future, I see courage. I think of what I would be like under such strain if our roles were reversed. The magnanimity of this woman staggers me. Her face remains serene throughout our time together.

As our gathering came to closure, those who had unburdened themselves to us in the very telling of their stories seemed relieved in giving us a firsthand understanding of their afflictions. They begged us to carry their stories back to the United States. They said to us, "Tell your people back home what you have seen and heard from us. Tell them we are here and don't forget us." Although their stories touch the soul deeply, there is no comparison to the shocking witness their physical presence gives. Their bodies, permanently maimed, are the visual testament to war's horror. The vision is unforgettable.

Hunger Stalks the Land

A revered elder in Gulu once took my hand in his and looked straight into my eyes, saying, "With the war came the hunger."

I remember having been told repeatedly that Acholiland was one of the most fertile regions in all of East Africa. Before the war, the industrious Acholi people were exporting foodstuffs to southern Uganda and Kenya. No one died of hunger because the Acholi were able to care for one another. This war reduced them to beggars forced to rely on the UN World Food Program for food rations enough to stay alive.

One summer afternoon, I was sitting on the front porch of the Comboni convent in Gulu relaxing with Sister Lena, an eighty-year-old Italian missionary. We were drinking lemonade and laughing when suddenly a small, twelve-year-old boy appeared under the archway that leads on to the porch. He had crutches on both sides of him for support. He was walking in very slow steps, more scuffling like an old man than walking with the energy of a young boy. Sister Lena's face lit up with the broadest of smiles and the boy squealed with joy. The boy's name was Sam Obita.

Sam was a patient at St. Mary's Hospital in Gulu. He secretly

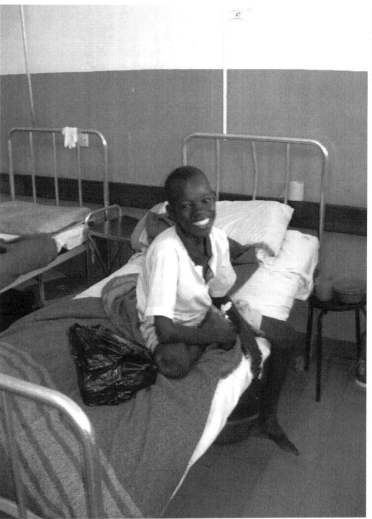

Sam Obita

snuck out of the hospital that summer afternoon in order to ask Sister Lena for a favor. He convinced an older boy with a motorcycle to transport him to the convent, assuring the boy that he could pay him for his service. He would rely on Sister Lena. She was known to have a heart that could deny no one a kindness. Sam needed food. Sam had not eaten in a very long time, despite the fact that he was a patient at a hospital. Strange events such as these mark reality in this war zone.

In this very hungry African city, as in many of the less-developed parts of the world, hospitals do not routinely provide meals as is done elsewhere. The families of the patients are responsible for providing the food and the bedding. Sam's father died of AIDS when Sam was still a toddler, too young to have any conscious memory of him. His mother also had died of AIDS when he was ten years old. He had a grandmother who was genuinely struggling to take care of him, but she frequently succumbed to the temptation to escape into alcohol to dull the sad memories. When she drank, she also forgot Sam.

This young boy is one of those people who everyone immediately likes; Sam's good spirit is always in evidence. When Sam was ten years old, he was the primary caregiver for his mother as she was dying. At night, he would tie a long string to one of her fingers and to one of his fingers and sleep under his mother's bed. If she needed anything during the night hours, water or the bedpan, all she had to do was tug on that string and Sam would quickly get up and help her.

Sam contracted the HIV virus from his parents. That was the reason he was a patient at the hospital. He was being treated for AIDS-related and hunger-related illnesses. Sam was terribly thin and very weak; the only thing strong about him was his character.

I helped escort Sam back to the hospital. He was by then too weak to walk so I went in search of a wheel chair. When none was found, I decided to carry him to his dormitory. I placed him on my shoulders and we raced through the hospital compound as Sam laughed uncontrollably. He acted like a child on a ride at an amusement park. He delighted in the thrill of moving fast and garnering the attention of the many onlookers. I promised him I would visit him every day while I was in Gulu.

Before the war, a host of diseases were prevalent in Gulu, but such hunger was unimaginable. Sam Obita succumbed to his illness, dying in mid-August 2005. To what extent the hunger this war brought contributed to his dying young is hard to determine. What is perfectly clear is that no child ought to live or die without enough food or love—and war makes it all the more uncertain that these treasures can be given by parents to their young.

Encounters with the Displaced of This War

All of northern Uganda is in chaos, and its youth know better than anyone else the calculated cruelty that has become commonplace. Fear and hopelessness are the rhythm of life, and many no longer know what this bizarre conflict is about or how it began. When native Ugandans are asked why this war continues to wage on in their homeland, most point to ancient grievances, Africa's history of militarized politics and interference by Uganda's northern neighbor, Sudan, which in the past supported the LRA with money and safe haven.

Since 1996, the government has undertaken a forced displacement of most of the population of northern Uganda. Nearly 1.6 million people—80 percent of whom are children and women—have been herded into vastly overcrowded camps for Internally Displaced People (IDP camps). This strategy was intended as a temporary measure in order to isolate the rebels. More than a decade later, this plan continues to wreak havoc on the local population, more a curse than a strategy for safety.

The living conditions I witnessed in the camps are shockingly inhuman. People wait in line for many hours to fill a single container of water. Many tell me they have stopped bathing altogether; the water is just too precious for anything but cooking and drinking. Inadequate sanitation and a total lack of privacy add to the frustration of everyday life. The gravest and most long-term danger is severe malnourishment. The best estimates suggest that upward of 40 percent of children less than five years of age have seriously stunted growth due to malnutrition, which will have an effect on their health for the rest of their lives. Many die in infancy; these camps have one of the worst infant mortality rates in the world.

There is a moral degradation here, a spirit of defeatism unlike anything I have ever witnessed. A government report from early 2005 estimated that one thousand people were dying weekly in the IDP camps. This staggering deathtoll is higher than even the number of weekly deaths in the ongoing genocide in Darfur, Sudan, reminding us that this is humanity's neglected tragedy. Suicides mount. It is highest among young mothers, who despair at their inability to provide for their young. In August 2005, thirteen mothers committed suicide in Pabbo Camp alone. Over the years, the children of northern Uganda have reached the sad realization that their parents, confined to the IDP camps, are no longer able to fulfill normal parental responsibilities. Mothers and fathers struggle and fail in providing their offspring with food, education, health care, and above all, safety from the rebels.

Uganda's Night Commuters

As marauding rebels are most active at night, having attacked both IDP camps and family huts in rural villages, the children live in great fear. They know that the rebels target them—they want young recruits at any price. This has led to thousands of them leaving their parents nightly to walk to the town centers where it is safer. They have been dubbed the "night commuters," commuting every single night from home to a safer place to lodge. Once in town, they sleep anywhere. Nearly forty thousand night commuters made the trek every evening in 2005. About one hundred boys and girls come to stay where I am lodged at St. Monica Girls' Tailoring Centre. The boys sleep in a hastily built metal room with straw mattresses. On one of my first nights at St. Monica's School, I was happy to discover that the St. Egidio Community was providing a simple plate of food for each of these youths whenever possible. A sixteen-year-old boy named Brian Oketayot noticed me sitting by the fire at suppertime without a plate of food. He sat down next to me, washed my hands and offered me half of his plate of beans and rice. That young teenager touched my soul with that simple yet courageous act of sharing.

It is obvious to me that all that the children want is to sleep safely in their own homes with their parents, enough food for the day, and the promise of a chance to build a more peaceful and humane world than the one given to them in their childhood.

Archbishop Odama, a keen observer of the destruction this war has brought to his children, decided in June 1998 to find a more

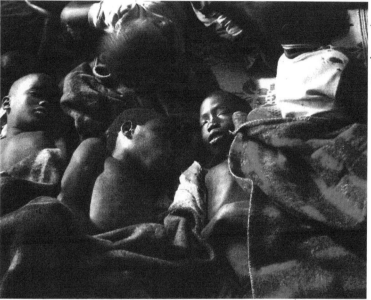

Night commuters sleeping safely on a floor

concrete and visible way to be in solidarity with the night commuters. One day he simply decided to join them. Quietly he left his residence one early evening with only a blanket under his arms and the determination to love the flock entrusted to him by Providence. A stream of night commuters was making their way on the streets to the Gulu bus park to sleep in relative safety. He simply entered into their company. "These are my colleagues, my fellow night commuters," he remarked with a smile to bystanders puzzled by the sight. For four consecutive nights, and many times thereafter, he became a frequent companion to those too frightened to stay home because home isn't a safe place.

What did he learn from this act of solidarity? He discovered first-hand the heavy toll this war is extracting from its youngest victims. He felt what it is like to sleep on the hard surface, often rugged and wet, the silence of the night interrupted with the nonstop sound of throngs of children coughing. The repeated night exposure makes many of the children sick. Since their bellies are often empty the kid's dream of breakfast and the promise of peace. The words of the suffering Job come to my mind: "The night drags on; I am filled with restlessness until the dawn, and I wonder: 'When will it be day?'" (Job 7:3-4).

These children spend long nights desiring two of life's treasured possessions, basic human rights that ought to be denied to no child: food and family. All across our world millions upon millions of children are gifted with food and family as part of their everyday experience. These necessities and the nurture they provide are so readily available that they could not imagine life without them. Not so in this war zone. Irony abounds: never before in human history has there been so much discussion across the globe, at the highest levels, about the rights of children, while at the same time these children suffer in silence and obscurity, denied almost everything essential for a truly human life.

I spent many memorable hours in the company of the night commuters who gather at St. Monica's. I found it energizing to be in their company. I was awestruck by the paradox that these youths who possessed practically nothing were more abundantly rich in spirit than most anyone I had encountered in my extensive travels around the world. I learned many lessons of life from them—preeminently, embrace the future. Amid tragedy after tragedy these children refuse to stop believing that tomorrow holds a promise of a better day. The number one request the night commuters gave to me was, "Father, help me find school fees so that I can stay in school." They know, at a very tender age, that education is the key that unlocks the door to the future.

The children start to arrive at dusk, as the Ugandan sky turns burnt red. They come in small groups, clusters of five or six at a time, the older ones holding the hands of small toddlers. These night commuters, who gathered here to escape the fear that they will be the next victims of this ongoing war, find a new mode of being once they walk through the protective gate at the entrance to St. Monica's. You can practically see their spirits become buoyant, happy to end their day safe in one another's company—singing and praying together.

They feel protected at St. Monica's; it has the highest wall in the city. Here they are free to be children again. Here they sleep under mosquito netting provided by the UN agency for children, UNICEF. Here the Community of St. Egidio, while providing something warm to eat before bedtime, also provides the semblance of normalcy. They play games and they pray the rosary together. Here the smiles and the encouragement of the sisters make a mother's love feel a little closer.

There is no television—there isn't even electricity much of the time. But the children sense themselves wealthy because they have the gift of one another. Some evenings they put on skits to entertain one another. At times they will stand outside the convent on the property and serenade the Sacred Heart sisters, who are so like mothers to them. There is visible gratitude on the faces of these youngsters for the sisters, who have opened their school's compound and their hearts to them. Every night they recite several decades of the rosary in their native language, Acholi, led by one of the older boys. They sing to their patron, St. Daniel Comboni, and place themselves under his strong protection. This Italian bishop and missionary, the first bishop of Khartoum, is famous for having remarked: "I have but one regret: that I have only one life to give for Africa."

Before the war, dusk in Acholiland used to be a time eagerly anticipated by all the members of the family. The work of the day was accomplished. It was now the cherished time for *wang oo*, the fireplace, the time to gather around a fire as a family to share relaxing and intimate moments. As the sun set one could hear the sounds of merriment and delight, the playful laughter of children filled the night air. Songs and drums echoed their melodies for all to take pleasure in. Love songs abounded. A favorite verse that the boys would sing to their sweethearts: "How short is the night with the one my heart loves" accompanied by the sound of the *nanga*. Children sing: "*Min latin do, tedo I dye wor*," that is, "My mother is cooking at night. . . ." In the dry season, one could lie down on the ground and gaze up at the full moon and the spectacularly starlit sky, which would make a magical scene.

The elders used this special time of the day to pass on the tribal traditions to their offspring. Ancient tales, proverbs, and the wise advice and legends about those who lived long ago were passed down to the next generation. What was imparted at *wang oo* was expected not only to be listened to seriously by the children but also to be memorized and ultimately interiorized. Many elders now fear that curtailing this beloved tradition for over twenty years because of insecurity has permanently damaged Acholi culture in an irreparable way.

Now, dusk is the time for children to find a hiding place from rebels. The sound of gunfire is so familiar to the children that even the youngest of them can distinguish whether the sound is mortar, rocket-propelled grenades, or machine gunfire. Trying to sleep is itself at times a hopeless task when apprehension is on the faces of everyone around you.

My friend Father Carlos Rodriguez, a Spanish missionary from Madrid, has spent numerous nights with the children in solidarity with their plight. He writes in his journal: "If you are lucky that the rebels are not waking you up with their guns, rain and storms will do it. The children rush to the already packed shelter of the bus park and spend the night just standing because there is no space. Others are so exhausted that they just continue lying down and getting all wet. Sanitation and filthiness is another problem too hard to describe. As I try to get at least a nap I am awoken by a long disturbing cry nearby. I pull myself up and I realize that I am the only one reacting. There in the dark there is a child who is having nightmares. No need to be alarmed. Every few minutes another child will utter a similar cry that pierces me to the heart. Dreaming of death and terror when you are only seven years old strikes me as a world gone mad."

In my childhood I had one recurring nightmare—it would come to me after watching my favorite film, *The Wizard of Oz*. This was a film every child in the United States looked forward to seeing once a year, even if it meant a sleepless night would follow. The Wicked Witch of the West seemed completely real to me and I feared that she could somehow abduct me like she kidnapped Dorothy. I would learn as an adult that I was not alone in my childhood fears. Tens of thousands of American youth were sent into nightmarish episodes every year after viewing this compelling film. Just the way she looked had the power to send me into a frightened panic. This person, the wickedest I had ever encountered, had seemingly one desire—to destroy Dorothy and anyone courageous enough to stand with her. The lines of reality and make believe were blurred for me. My parents alone provided the assurance of my protection and safety. As I met hundreds upon hundreds of Ugandan orphans, who walk into their future without the loving protection of parental love, I am fearful for them; they are walking into an uncertain and hazardous future.

Last night, close to forty million of our sisters and brothers did not sleep at home because home is not a safe place to be anymore. In all my life experiences, home is where I have fled to, not from, in times of threat or insecurity.

About half of that number, close to twenty million people, continues to inhabit their own nation but not their homes because of insecurity. They have been given the appellation Internally Displaced Persons, and their primitive, temporary new homes are IDP camps. Those who have crossed national borders, fleeing the violence in the homeland, are commonly referred to as refugees. The UN High Commissioner for Refugees has special responsibilities for their welfare. A staggering one and a half million people became internally displaced because of the LRA rebellion across northern Uganda.

On a walk through Pagak IDP camp, home to more than five thousand people, most of whom are children, I step into a world of contrast. There is squalor and deprivation everywhere. The contrast I perceive is not in the harshness of the living conditions—everyone here is in the same sort of depressing circumstances. But in a matter of just two minutes, I encounter two contrasting groups of young men. One group appears to have given up on the future; the other is busily planning to embrace it.

The first is clearly intoxicated while it is still early in the day. They have found their preferred form of escapism—alcohol. It appears that

Piero Paul Rubangakene

A young boy fighting an imaginary enemy

when even the most basic and rudimentary requirements of life are lacking the procurement of alcohol can still top the priority list.

These young men are drinking *ajono*, a homemade, millet-based brew, trying to escape the misery with an unbelievably cheap and available alcohol. It is produced in the camp for sale in the camp. As several of these inebriated men shake my hand they refuse to let go. This has never happened to me before and I am practically forced to fight to get my hand free. They laugh loudly and slur their words. Their bloodshot eyes look vacant. It is still only 10:30 AM.

My escort tells me that this drinking to the point of intoxication is like an everyday ritual for these men in the camps. Along with playing cards, gambling, and numerous games of chance, they wile away the day. In contrast, the women always seem occupied with the everyday chores of life, which remain unavoidable. Some groups of men get drunk three times a day, every day. In a community hut where some are gathered to share drinks, there is country western music blaring. It fills the morning air.

The second group of young men I encounter immediately after greeting our intoxicated friends seems very animated, their energy level high. Some have brought their spouses and young children to a morning meeting held under the shade of a large tree. I would learn that Caritas International had organized this small, but highly dedicated group. They were to receive seeds for the next planting, concentrating on onions and tomatoes. They are promised at this gathering that Caritas will provide skilled persons who will show them new, more efficient ways of tending to their crops. Everyone agrees that that would be a most welcomed initiative—this could propel their project forward.

Everyone in this second group is high spirited. They can already see a future after the chaos that currently engulfs their lives. I immediately sense their leadership skills. I say to myself: "These folks could build a new Uganda after this war." The war has shattered the social fabric of hundreds of thousands of families and the rebuilding of family life will require strong leadership. I think I met some of those leaders in this group.

My attention is drawn to the activity of the women in the camp, old and young. I watch curiously as an elderly woman prepares the yeast she has grown for sale. It is destined to be used to make beer or *ajono* for the men. I am told that she will be happy with the small amount of cash she will earn from it. Most women here are engaged in some way with food production. I am struck again with the realization that in many places in the world the procurement of food is an all-consuming task for the day. A band of young women are sun-drying grains, others are sifting the chaff from what is good. Every woman I encounter at Pagak, without exception, was doing something productive: childcare, food production, tending to household necessities, or procuring water, firewood, and oil for cooking.

On hundreds of doors to the huts in the IDP camps I see the letters *USA* in patriotic red, white, and blue. I ask my escort why so many residents of this camp place my country's name on the entrance to their home. It seems so bizarre. Even as I ask the question I sense there is a very simple explanation that eludes me. He enlightens me: "These doors are made from large, discarded tin containers holding vegetable oil for cooking. It is donated to us by USAID and it bears the insignia of the donor nation." I am reminded that nothing useful in this region of the world is ever thrown away. In North America, if everyone ate all the food that we throw away callously, it is estimated that all North Americans would weigh 337 pounds each. Here at Pagak IDP camp even the containers that once held oil for cooking are not thrown away—they become the front doors of the homes these people inhabit.

7

Kony and Koresh

Shocking Similarities

I t would seem to Americans that the nightmares unleashed on children in the LRA are a world far away from us and could never happen here in the heartland of America. That is simply not true; to some extent, they have already occurred.

The lifestyle and cultic practices of Joseph Kony, the supreme commander of the LRA in East Africa, are shockingly similar to an American counter-part, David Koresh. David Koresh was at the helm of the Davidian Cult in Waco, Texas, before this group's disastrous standoff with the FBI on April 19, 1993. That fateful day, Koresh and seventy-six Branch Davidians perished in an inferno after refusing to surrender to U.S. government authorities.

Kony and Koresh both believed that God spoke directly to them; both stockpiled weapons in an attempt to claim power by force for themselves; both engaged in frequent, rampant sexual encounters with the female members of their group. Koresh and Kony both promised their followers that they, and they alone, could reveal the deepest designs of God for them and their destiny. Both appealed to God as the one who gave legitimacy to their bizarre and brazen form of leadership.

Mount Carmel, the compound housing the Branch Davidians in Waco, was a place festering with child abuse and violent extremism in much the same manner as the LRA camps. Both Koresh and Kony were taking young girls to their beds as if by right. They acted as if all females of the world were destined to be submissive to them, while at the same time ordering all the young men in their charge to remain celibate until given sexual license from them. Koresh and Kony each sought complete mastery over as many children as they could recruit and indoctrinate into their cults. Both Kony and Koresh, each a megalomaniac in their own right, preached a vision of violent confrontation with the government. Their own demonic control over their followers was absolutely essential in the battle.

Since reasoning adults would be far more discerning and difficult to manipulate, both Kony and Koresh understood that their survival was all about the children. David Koresh taught the children a mantra: "We are soldiers in the army. We've got to fight. Some day we have to die. We have to hold up the bloodstained banner. We have to hold it up until we die."

The children of Waco and the children of the LRA were not allowed to have contact with anyone outside the cult. In this way, coercion was more easily accomplished. Kony and Koresh were always adamant that no outside voice reach their followers since that might fracture the illusion they had built up to entrap the children. These charismatic men thirsted for blind obedience from those not yet gifted with enough life experience and education to make informed decisions. The center of their movement could not have held if not for blind or coerced obedience. Joseph Kony has proven to be an intractable foe to more than thirty thousand youths who have fallen prey to his calculated cruelty. Koresh has had a demonlike influence on far fewer numbers of children.

Joseph Kony is a former altar boy and his father was a catechist. He is frequently described by those who have lived alongside him in the bush as a good-looking, charismatic man, who is fond and protective of the multitude of children born of his enslaved wives. Unverifiable estimates of the number of children fathered by Kony are over one hundred children. He appears to nearly everyone who has heard his speeches or rantings to be endowed with magical powers. He has been compared to Adolph Hitler in his eerie ability to stir up a crowd with spirited oratory and to convince them of the worthiness of his crusade. Kony is revered like a messiah in this insurgency movement, which is more like a cult than an army. Of himself, he has claimed, "God can confirm that I am an embodiment and personification of the Holy Spirit."

While the force of his personal charisma has swayed many people who have observed Joseph Kony's actions, personally, I am certain he does not possess any magical powers. I do not doubt that he has carefully crafted the appearance of being gifted by God with extraordinary gifts and supernatural powers. Kony desperately needs people to believe he has divine resources. It is a cold, calculated deception. This controlling deception makes him not only devious but far more dangerous as well.

The undiscerning children are the ones most readily won over. The deception needed to sway them is more limited than adults, who are less likely to see the magical and fanciful parading as the spiritual. They will be his victims because he is masterful in exerting power over young and vulnerable persons.

Life as a Rebel's Wife

On July 1, 2007, I spent the entire morning with a fascinating woman named Margaret Abalo. She is a very attractive young mother, who has given birth to four children, one of whom died in early childhood. The father of all her children is Joseph Kony.

When Margaret was just sixteen years old, she was walking in the early evening on the road toward Awer Market outside of Gulu. Rebels ambushed Margaret and her friends. That night began a very lengthy captivity for her in which her physical attractiveness singled her out from the beginning for special treatment, a treatment no woman would ever want. Of the eight abductees taken that night, all were released after just days, except for Margaret and another girl.

Realizing her beauty, the rebels tried to take her immediately to Joseph Kony but he had already left the area for another district. She was then kept under armed guard at that location for more than two months. When Joseph Kony arrived and saw her, he ordered her to be transferred to one of his houses. Since one of Kony's wives was pregnant, Margaret was given the task to help with the household chores and to give assistance to this woman.

As I listened to Margaret, I was stunned by the commodification of life being described to me. Margaret was seen as a valuable commodity to the rebels. She was an object and a prize; they recognized this the very first moment they looked at her. What an assault it is on a person's dignity to look on him or her primarily as an object of pleasure for others. Joseph Kony's choice to use young boys to fight for him and to use young girls as sex slaves demonstrates just how entrenched the commodification of life has been in the LRA brigade; it is their way of life.

During my interview with her, I asked if only the most attractive girls were sent to Kony. Margaret blushed and answered, "Yes. They are chosen according to his choice, when they are young and beautiful." Margaret went on to tell me that she was "investigated" throughout her first full month in Kony's home. During that time she did not have sexual relations with him. Commanders repeatedly questioned her about her personal life. They wanted to know whether she had ever engaged in witchcraft and they asked questions about her character and family background. She did not realize it then, but she was being interrogated to see if she would be a worthy consort for the supreme commander of the LRA, Joseph Kony.

How perverse the LRA rebels had become. They wanted to protect the madman Kony from any contamination coming from abducted, innocent youths, who were somehow not perfect in their eyes.

All, especially Kony himself, deemed Margaret suitable. If you were chosen as a wife of Kony's, and Margaret personally met forty-five other wives of his, you were to have sexual relations with no one else. Indeed, the others in the LRA never questioned this out of fear of what might befall them if they shared a girl with Kony. On the other hand, Kony could give one of his girls away if he grew tired of her. They were his own possession to do with as he saw fit. In the more than thirteen years that Margaret was with the LRA, Joseph Kony never grew tired of her.

Daily life was drudgery for Margaret. In the early years, she was kept busy cooking for the soldiers. She became a victim of frequent beatings. One of the senior wives would occasionally make false reports about the younger wives, motivated by jealousy, and the accused wives were beaten. She suffered from dysentery and gunshot wounds. In one battle, she was caught in the crossfire and sustained bullet wounds in both the chest and the foot.

Margaret was an eyewitness to the way Joseph Kony pretended to know the future and tried to manipulate his soldiers. She told how he would receive scouting reports about the movements of Ugandan government forces, and as they neared, he would predict that a battle was about to start. He would tell his soldiers that if they had faith they would escape death and if they did not have faith they would surely die. He claimed to hear all of this directly from God. The children believed every word and sensed that God had indeed spoken to Kony about an impending battle.

Margaret wants all to know that she never loved Kony. It was the vulnerability thrust on her by the condition of her captivity that alone forced her to accept Kony as a husband. The only other option was to be executed for her refusal.

In July 2003, the Ugandan government soldiers managed a surprise attack on Kony's hideout in southern Sudan and came very close to capturing him. At the last minute, Kony jumped into a hole and avoided detection. Margaret seized the moment when all was in confusion to race in the direction of northern Uganda.

She walked for a solid month, bearing in her arms her one-month-old son. Finally, government forces found her and took her and her baby to a reception center, where she was joyfully reunited with her other two children, who had escaped all on their own.

This fourth child of hers, her last born, she named Daniel Comboni. I find it curious that Daniel Comboni may be the only name in this region of the world more well known than that of the child's father, Joseph Kony. St. Daniel Comboni, an Italian missionary to Africa in the nineteenth century, spread the Christian message of love, forgiveness, and peace in a heroic way. His picture is everywhere in east central Africa. Three-year-old Daniel Comboni is handsome, with eyes that flash intelligence. I wonder what his future may hold.

In July 2006, President Museveni announced that he wanted to send a delegation of formerly captured persons to see Kony at his hideout in the Garamba National Park in the eastern region of the Democratic Republic of the Congo. Kony had made statements in which he expressed fear for his former wives and his children. It was Kony's belief that they were being mistreated back home in Uganda after they fled his company. Indeed, Kony feared that members of his family might fall victim to revenge killings.

Margaret Abalo was one of the first to be asked to be a member of this delegation, and she said yes. She reports that Kony was very interested in how his children were doing and whether they were really alive and well. The delegation stayed with Kony three days. On the final day, Margaret grew restless and fearful. She doubted whether Kony would really allow her to walk away free or if, at the last minute, she alone would be prevented from leaving. Once again in his company, the control and dominance Kony held over her resurfaced again in a very physical way.

The Ultimate Commodification of Life

Kony has made promises to his abducted youths that he will provide for their needs and reward their victories. The most striking reward offered in the LRA ranks was to be given one's own "wife," a euphemism for sex slave, female servant, or plaything. I learned of the gruesome details surrounding being given such a trophy by a series of extensive interviews with a newly rescued former LRA soldier. Santos was himself a recipient of Kony's way of rewarding loyalty. He explained to me how the young in Kony's power are manipulated to such an extent that whether they want to be given a sex slave or not, Kony convinces everyone that it is vital that they comply. Noncompliance in the LRA always leads to death—sooner or later.

Santos was kidnapped when he was fifteen years old. He quickly came to know that obedience to Kony and his chief lieutenants was the only route to survival. He was as compliant and submissive to the will of the leaders as all the others, but inwardly he railed against them. After five years in forced fighting in the LRA, Kony deemed it an opportune time to reward this young man and his comrades for their obedient behavior. The reward, in essence, would be sexual license.

It was a Friday afternoon and Santos was now in the summer of his twentieth year. He and nine other young men approximately his age were summoned together. They were told that they had achieved a level of accomplishment and excellence in serving the cause of the LRA. Appreciation was now to be shown to them for their good work. At that precise moment eleven young girls, mostly teenagers, were brought forward. The commander spoke: "Divide these girls among you, one per person. On Sunday night, the one who is not chosen, that girl will be executed." This method of distributing the captured girls was designed especially to make them compliant, desirous of being chosen as a "wife."

The Lord's Resistance Army—adults and children

Santos did not want to be given a wife. It was not an option for him, and he felt he would be executed if he did not accept. The LRA leaders want their soldiers to propagate the brigade with their off-spring, children who could be trained to help in the war effort from very early on in their lives. Imagine children being born for the express intention of waging guerilla warfare. This is the sheer commodification of life: treating persons as mere objects to exploit and use.

Santos spoke of how he felt that he was not emotionally ready to begin being sexually active. This was not the right time or place to begin a family. He was not particularly attracted to any of the girls brought before them. Still, in his particular situation, that decision was out of his hands. Kony had supreme powers in the LRA that penetrated deeply into the personal lives of his abducted recruits.

Santos and the girl he chose to be his wife had two children born to them while in the LRA. After having been rescued from the rebels, Santos feels a greater sense of moral obligation toward the children than toward their mother. He struggles today to help provide for their livelihood.

The attention of male fighters in the LRA appears, at least on the surface, to be fixed on two trophies bestowed upon them by those holding all the power: their girl and their gun—these are the possessions the boys are taught to prize most.

In the summer of 2007, the Russian army celebrated the birth, sixty years earlier, of the premier gun of the twentieth century—the Kalashnikov, known commonly as the AK-47. It was designed by Mikhail Kalashnikov, a Russian officer. This lethal automatic rifle is the weapon of choice for Africa's warlords and guerilla fighters. It is lightweight and easily slung over the shoulders of a ten-year-old boy. More than one hundred million AK-47 weapons have been manufactured since 1947. It has seven well-adjusted pieces and is considered by military experts to be one of the world's most efficient weapons.

The image of this gun is celebrated across the globe. Its image appears on the leaflets of Hezbollah guerrillas, on the Mozambican flag, and on the stamps of the tiny African nation of Burkina Faso. Nations and movements attribute their success to the battles they have fought chiefly with this weapon. The AK-47 is cheap. A new one can be purchased for only two hundred dollars, and in Africa's war zones and wherever trade in small arms abounds a used one can be found for as little as thirty dollars.

It was Santos who told me the most alarming tale I heard of life and death in the company of LRA rebels. It dealt with the chastisements carried out on any of the youths who panic in battle and simply drop their AK-47 and run away. The punishment immediately conveys to all that the gun is infinitely more valuable to the rebel brigade than the child soldier is. Child soldiers are easily replaceable; an AK-47 is not.

The armaments the LRA use are imported from beyond the African continent. Many weapons in the hands of child soldiers in East Africa were originally manufactured in Russia or other places thousands of miles away. But a new recruit, the next vulnerable child or teenager, can be kidnapped from right down the road. A gun or rocket-propelled grenade launcher must be purchased from extremely limited rebel resources and brought to the Ugandan battlefield from far away.

Santos recalled the sickening first time he saw a new recruit drop a gun and run from the battlefield. Rebels went in pursuit and captured him. They instantly turned on him, treating him worse than the enemy. This young person was executed in full view of all the others. The message was overpowering to all—do this and you will meet a similar violent end.

The level of violence against that child continued to escalate after his death. The others were ordered to cut his body into pieces and begin boiling the flesh. Each member of the brigade was ordered to eat part of the dead boy's body. By such extreme measures everyone knew their relative importance vis-à-vis an AK-47. The life of an individual has no value in and of itself. He or she gains value only as a commodity, and there are three valuable commodities in the war waged by the LRA: a boy soldier, a girl who can provide sexual services and birth children, and an AK-47. In the LRA everyone knew which commodity was most valuable.

Santos, against his will and against every human inclination, participated in this cannibalism out of fear of his own death. When questioned as to what human flesh tastes like, he retorted, "It tastes like nothing. I just ate it to satisfy the commander. I feared not to act on their every order. They would surely have killed me next if I did not comply."

In my priestly ministry in the diocese of Cleveland, I have been invited to the homes of hundreds of parishioners over the last quarter century to share a meal. Often during the course of these visits, the young people in these families show me the trophies they have amassed over the years. They were won at debate competitions, swimming meets, tennis tournaments, wrestling matches, Boy Scout and Girl Scout events, and various other kinds of competitions. The trophy is a confirmation of their excellence. It tells all who see it that there is a certain distinction evident in the performance of this young person and that he or she can be justifiably proud.

Santos was not at all proud of himself, or of his gun or his girl. Remorse is very evident in the tone of his voice and in his vacant eyes as he relates such tragic stories. I wonder how much regret a young life can handle before it becomes intolerable.

What message does the Christian faith bear for Santos, a young man so wounded and so remorseful? The virtue of hope compels us to believe that the worst things that have happened to us in our lives do not define who we are. The forgiveness of past wrongs and the possibility for new beginnings are not utopian ideals; rather, they are central to the message and teachings of Jesus Christ. Brother Jesus walked among us to make us new people of a new covenant, regardless of how tragic the road we have walked.

Our faith as Christians is biblical. So we must ask, What does our biblical tradition ask of us at this moment, in this painful situation? First and foremost is that we must feel compassion for all who have suffered the devastating consequences of the LRA war. This is truly a non-negotiable in our Christian faith. Bitterness, viciousness, a personal distancing of ourselves from this tragedy, or a refusal to forge a way to healing and forgiveness are not options for a disciple of Christ, who taught us that power lies not in conquering and vanquishing our enemy but in the forgiveness that only restorative justice can create.

Wallowing in remorse will not advance the call to rebuild Ugandan solidarity and create a more just society. Thousands of youths like Santos look for a way out of the bitterness that has settled deep in their spirits. Fortunately, many spiritual resources are found within the traditional beliefs of their culture. One particular Acholi cultural ritual designed to remove bitterness from the spirit may hold promise for a new day in northern Uganda.

Traditional Rituals of Healing

A first step in the current work being done to achieve peace in Uganda is to agree on an acceptable means of dealing with justice. Unlike many Western cultures, in the Acholi culture justice is not focused on punishment. Rather, restitution, repentance, and forgiveness form the basis for justice. This is the approach most desired by the people, including many of the victims of the rebel atrocities. While use of such a ritual may be difficult for the Western world to accept, it has deep roots and many layers of meaning for the tribes of northern Uganda.

There are many tribal rituals associated with forgiveness, healing, and cleansing throughout Africa and each has a purpose and a spiritual meaning. The people of northern Uganda live in a spiritual realm unlike any in our acquaintance. Current peace discussions most often turn to the ritual known as *mato oput*, a ritual for situations in which a killing, intentional or accidental, has taken place.

The typical first step in the traditional Acholi healing process is to separate the two sides, allowing time for emotions to subside. The two parties are brought together only when they can speak to each other without anger; the discussions that take place then must lead to reconciliation between victim and perpetrator, to genuine forgiveness and acceptance between the two clans as well as agreement on the appropriate form of restitution. Only when everything has been settled can the day-long ritual cleansing ceremony take place.

The final *mato oput* ceremony begins with the beating of a stick to symbolize future violence that might happen between the two clans (groups) in the absence of reconciliation. After this ritual action, the offending clan runs away, signifying the acceptance of guilt for the violent act of killing. Accepting blame is at the heart of the ritual, and without it there can be no further move toward healing. It is this acknowledgment that is the first and greatest gift of restitution for those who grieve.

The offending clan then provides a sheep, and the injured clan a goat. Each animal is cut in half, and the halves are exchanged in a gesture of unity that signifies a readiness to forgive and be forgiven, leading to reconciliation and wholeness. Next, the clans share in eating *boo mukwok,* greens that are said to have spoiled because of the long period of tension between the two parties. Eating these greens is another symbol of the readiness to reconcile.

Then the bitter juice of the *oput* tree is shared by a representative of each clan. Drinking this bitter red liquid represents the washing down of any bitter feelings between the two parties. The action of drinking is as full of meaning as the drink is itself. In sharing this drink from the same calabash, each person kneels before the cup with hands clasped behind their back. Then the two knock their heads together, bringing into unity that which had been separated, and then drink. Following this action, the ceremony focuses on the sharing of food between the clans as a first act of togetherness. First, the livers of the sheep and goat are cooked and eaten. The remaining bitter drink must then be consumed completely by both clans, freeing them to share a meal. On the day of the ceremony, all of the food prepared must be consumed in order for *mato oput* to be considered complete. This complete sharing represents the end of any bitterness between the two clans.

This ritual has limitations that have caused some to question the appropriateness of *mato oput* for the situation faced in Uganda. First, it is meant to be undertaken between two clans, with one making restitution to the other. This war, however, is so widespread and affects so many clans that it is difficult to conceive of a means of using *mato oput* in its traditional form. At the same time, the practice traditionally deals only with reconciliation after a killing. What then is to be done to deal with rapes, disfigurements, and kidnappings? Can the ritual be adapted to complete the process of reconciliation in these cases?

Other traditional rituals have been used as this war in Uganda has waged and come to a tentative and fragile peace. One of the most common is *nuono tong gweno,* or stepping on the egg. As victims and surrendering rebels return from the bush, this ritual provides a comforting message of welcome to those who consider returning home from the LRA.

Another ritual, *moyo kum,* is performed to cleanse the body of ill deeds. It has been used as a postconflict ritual in other areas of Africa and may also be beneficial in Uganda. A second cleansing ritual, *moyo piny,* can be performed on land that has seen the violence of war.

Finally, the ritual of *lwongo tipu* also seems particularly appropriate in dealing with the aftermath of LRA activities, since its purpose is to put to rest the spirit of a person who has disappeared. As noted above, many bodies of children were found in the bush, and the families of the many kidnapped and lost children of this war can find some spiritual peace and closure through this calling of their spirits.

Although these rites, filled with symbols and empty of punitive consequences, may seem ineffective to a world culture that favors imprisonment and focuses on punishment to effect justice, the sharing of the bitter root can be very powerful. The concept of two bitterly opposed clans coming together to drink from the same cup, often at the same time, becomes much more profound when imaging Joseph Kony performing this action with those so deeply wounded by his LRA. The level of forgiveness that must be present in the hearts of those performing this ritual action would be profound. Taken alone, the ceremonies may not seem sufficient, but the process of discussion that leads to the final cleansing rituals is one of Christian values and respect for the dignity of every human being.

No one has spoken more persuasively to me about what *mato oput*, the drinking of the bitter root, can accomplish in healing life's deepest wounds as retired Anglican Bishop MacLeod Baker Ochola. A close friend and chief collaborator with Archbishop Odama in the Acholi Religious Leaders Peace Initiative, Bishop Ochola's diocese of Kitgum has been an LRA stronghold that has experienced innumerable assaults and untold suffering since the beginning of this war. Bishop Ochola has devoted his life to the pursuit of peace for his people, no matter what the toll might be.

I first met him when we were both houseguests of Archbishop Odama. His gentle and gracious spirit and his warmth and vitality lit up the room. Later on, I learned that the war had taken a heavy toll on the bishop and his family and that his wife had been killed by landmines in 1997.

How does a grieving husband find the inner strength to forgive the murderers of his wife? How will the Acholi people find within themselves the capacity to forgive the rapes, tortures, and child abductions that have decimated their families and their homeland? How will Sunday Obote pardon those who stole his entire childhood from him when he was just seven years old? How will Oscar find the inner wherewithal to confront and forgive those who wiped out his entire family? To me, such a level of forgiveness seems nearly impossible.

Bishop Ochola embodies what the grace of restorative justice can achieve within one person and his culture. Ideals can be seen far more vividly in one person than in any theoretical discussion of justice and responsibility. Bishop Ochola believes that while the Acholi understanding of justice greatly differs from other cultures, it is far more biblical. Sacred scripture reveals a far more profound meaning of justice than can be legislated today. The biblical idea of justice represents fidelity to the demands of a relationship. The emphasis is not on the crime but on the breaking of a relationship and the moral call to restore and rebuild what has been broken.

Bishop Ochola helped me understand that *mato oput* is based on six interlocking principles: truth, mercy, justice, peace, restoration, and transformation. It is a process that builds on the initial moment of truth that is accompanied by the acceptance of responsibility. The offering of forgiveness is conditional in Acholi culture: *if you* accept responsibility, *if you* own your actions, victims will forgive and, indeed, must forgive you.

Will Joseph Kony ever be able to accept the truth about his particular role in the deaths of ten thousand children? That singular question holds the crux to the answer of whether or not the ritual of *mato oput* will ever succeed in bringing a sustained peace to this war-weary region of Africa.

Vincent Otti, one of Kony's highest ranking commanders, and supposedly a friend as well, was rumored to have been executed by the LRA leader in October 2007. At first Kony repeatedly denied these claims and fabricated stories about Otti's absence. Finally in January 2008, Kony admitted openly that his former friend was dead, and eyewitnesses confirmed that Otti died by a firing squad acting on Kony's direct orders. Kony himself, however, refuses to admit this fact. If acknowledging the execution of one man is so difficult for Kony, who claims to desire peace, how likely is he to admit the full truth about his war crimes, to acknowledge the kidnapping, mutilating, and killing of tens of thousands of youths? This truth—this acceptance of responsibility—is the mountain that stands between the Ugandan people and true peace.

8

The Path to Healing

Is Healing Possible for Child Soldiers?

A s I listen to the stories of formerly abducted children forced into war, I am awestruck by the level of violence inflicted on them. One has to wonder how much a young person can endure before collapsing into defeat and accepting their personal dark future as an inescapable fate. The psychological consequences alone of killing, at any age but in particular while you are still only a child, are staggering. I have often found myself bewildered and overcome with grief as the victims told me their stories.

The LRA is in the business of guerilla warfare and, by and large, has been one of the most highly successful guerilla insurgency movements in the world. To what do they owe their success? The use of abducted children and teens as soldiers has been one of their main strategic choices in this gruesome business. It has proven to have had innumerable benefits that the rebels have seized.

Why is it that, in the end, they targeted teenagers and younger boys deliberately, in fact, almost exclusively? Is it just for the most obvious and apparent reason that no mature, discerning person is likely to be won over to their cause because of the vile and always ferocious means they employ in pursuit of power?

I think it is more complex than that which readily appears on the surface. It is also subtly joined to the widely accepted belief that in all warfare an eighteen-year-old generally makes a better soldier than a thirty- or forty-year-old does. This is why we universally ask that the younger among us go to fight the battle. This is why we insist that the young do what we, the older and more cautious, are unwilling or unable to do.

**Orphans of war cutting grass around
St. Joseph Cathedral in Gulu, Uganda**

Indisputably, their bodies are reaching their peak of physical prowess. What is also true and underappreciated is that their powers of reasoning, linked directly to certain areas of the brain, are not yet fully developed. Thus several factors collide into a perfect storm: vulnerable, pliable youth, who are physically strong yet unable to grasp the full and dire ramifications of their actions, are inordinately swayed by the evil conditions rampant in the LRA. As the LRA war raged on, their commanders felt compelled to target youths fourteen years and younger precisely because they were viewed as far less autonomous than their older counterparts, more dependent on the adult world around them, less capable of distinguishing right from wrong, and far more prone to imitate the adults who wield absolute power and influence over them and who would force them to do their bidding.

Grace Akallo was a fifteen-year-old student at St. Mary's, a Catholic boarding school in Aboke, northern Uganda, when she was kidnapped by LRA rebels along with 138 of her classmates on the night of October 10, 1996.[1] Upon escaping after seven torturous months in guerilla warfare, this courageous and articulate young woman has offered one of the most powerful eyewitness accounts of life in the LRA.[2] She has chronicled how the rebels exert tremendous powers of coercion over the children and condition them to want to do the same monstrous acts they see the LRA soldiers perform. Grace tells us: "There was one commander who, if he was not killing someone, was not happy. When he was killing someone, he was happy. People would start crying that they wanted to kill someone. One eighteen-year-old boy came out of the line crying that he wanted to kill someone. This boy—they would give him ten children. He'd say he was taking them for a bath. He'd kill five, and only five would come back."[3] While in the custody of people bent on death and destruction, these youth were schooled to want to do the same. Life in the LRA appears as one long training exercise in killing.

Youth abducted into the LRA are still generally developing in their emotional and mental capacities, even if their bodies appear fully mature. The region of the brain known as the prefrontal cortex is still maturing for people their age. This is the brain region that helps adults to predict the consequences of their actions. It is located in the frontmost area of the brain and is the last region to be fully developed. This finally happens for most people sometime in late adolescence or even into early adulthood. The amygdala, part of the limbic system, located more deeply within the center of the brain, is that part of the brain associated with gut responses and survival instincts. It develops earlier in life, as it is needed to regulate basic bodily functions, emotions, and drives.

What enables a teen to march up a hill, anticipating a deadly skirmish, and still be willing to proceed? It is the fight-or-flight response that is modulated by the more developed limbic system. It is the hard-wired, automatic response that the body possesses in order to survive. In this gut response adrenaline flows all throughout the body in a ferocious way, preparing for the immediate moment of frenzy soon to break out. Because of it, rational thinking becomes even more limited than it already is in these youths. At the same time, endorphins are spontaneously released and act as an immediate and natural painkiller. These chemical compounds, found naturally in the body, resemble opiates in their function. They create an uncanny ability to produce a sense of well-being even amid the deadliest of dangers. There is exhilaration in the face of pain, overwhelming stress, and imminent danger.

Fully mature adults routinely rely on their use of the prefrontal cortex; juveniles cannot because theirs isn't fully developed yet. They likely do not appreciate the full ramification of their actions, the vast and future consequences of their deeds. Reflection and deliberation come with the reasoning of maturity, if one lives long enough to be gifted with these attributes. A full appreciation of the consequences of their actions eludes teens. That is why they are more willing than adults to be placed in perilous situations in which others would refuse to go. That is why, when there is nothing but danger surrounding them, they may act not in a reasoned capacity but from gut responses based principally, almost solely, on the will to live. A more mature person would seek every avenue to avoid being placed in such a precarious condition. A more mature person would fully comprehend what is at stake in remaining in the company of these rebels who are intent on death and destruction.

In the face of continual exposure to the horrors of abduction, violence, and killing, the brains of these youths remain constantly saturated with adrenaline, which promotes survival, but actually hinders the maturation of the prefrontal brain areas during one of the most significant times of brain development. The maturing of the prefrontal cortex and the ability to make choices and control emotions is a vast learning experience, colored by the experiences and lessons of daily life. A world in constant stress and turmoil will surely help define the very identity of these children, their consciences, and their whole view of themselves and their world.

Since the brains of juveniles are not yet fully developed, they cannot, in any legitimate way, be held to adult standards. That is why in the United States and in most other nations there is a juvenile justice system separate from the adult court. Children and adolescents differ from adults in multiple ways: biologically, emotionally, and spiritually they are at different stages of development from each other and must never be judged or evaluated by the same standards. Still, in our day, many would insist that those who commit a violent crime be judged by their actions solely, regardless of their age, their reasoning capacity, or the circumstance that prompted or even forced them to act. What most impels the youth within the LRA to act is the fear of death made clear to them in the commands of their subjugators: "Kill or be killed!"

It would appear that a more nuanced appreciation of what is at stake when children are forced to kill would insist that they, the child soldiers, be judged by a more comprehensive appreciation of the moral act. The act itself, the circumstances, and the intention of the acting agent form an interlocking and single unit. This appreciation eludes far too many in our day. Child soldiers have diminished rationality and only incipient autonomy, two crucial considerations when making a moral judgment concerning personal culpability.

How we judge these youths will be a vitally important component to their healing process. First and foremost, they need to know and to experience that they are always our children. Prolonged isolation from everyone who has ever loved them has had a chilling effect on these youths—they feel all alone in the world. We need to reach out to them and show them that the lies they were fed while in the LRA about how they would be hated and severely punished by their communities if they dared to return home were concocted stories. They were nothing more than ploys to keep them from attempting escape. Still the challenges of coming home are practically beyond telling for many of these children, who all too often do experience scorn, ridicule, and in not a few cases, even the rejection they had been warned by the rebels to expect.

If a child abducted at age seven returns back home at age seventeen, he or she is a completely different person, who is nearly unrecognizable to their families. Returning LRA child soldiers are, in some households, more feared than welcomed by their families. The rebels have made great inroads in their young lives as they train these children to be like them: fiercely aggressive, combative, and unfeeling toward others.

Still, success stories abound and must be replicated. One strategy that appears to be working for many former LRA child fighters is, after a relatively brief time of reunion at home, resuming their schooling in a boarding situation. There trained teachers and mentors can help them negotiate some of the troubling times that lie ahead. This has certainly been the case with Sunday Obote who seems to flourish more in the Catholic boarding school he has attended than he did at home, where he was alone with his mother. She has grown old and unable to nurture him as she did when he was younger. She is thrilled that others are taking the initiative to help get her son the kind of assistance he needs to reclaim his life.

For the child soldiers of the LRA now in newly found freedom, life is all about reclaiming their humanity. There are two stages to true freedom for these youths: the outside fight and the inside fight. They no longer need to physically fight others in order to simply survive; those days are in the past. But it is a long and arduous journey to win the inner fight of being released from the demons they carry from the battlefields in their minds, hearts, and spirits. To reclaim one's soul is an altogether different prospect. There is a universal need for love that has been utterly denied to them while in the LRA, leaving a cavernous hole in their souls.

The human being is the most complex of all God's creation, and the human brain is the most complex of human organs. At the same time that youth in the LRA are at a diminished capacity for reflection because their brains are not fully developed, their brains are well suited to store millions of memories, and many of these are tragic. The brain clings to certain information because at one time it was deemed vital to the body's survival. Those memories, permanently lodged in the brain, can return to haunt the children of the LRA. Memories of the innumerable and unspeakable crimes that child soldiers are forced, under penalty of death, to perpetrate in the bush are all retained.

Pictures of precisely what happened to them and to their victims while caught up in guerilla warfare are stored in their memory. These images come alive to them in flashbacks. They haunt their dreams, in the daytime and in the nighttime. These painful images of past horrors persist, lodged in the child soldier's brain. Such memories surface of their own will. They slowly start to form the foundations of a learned reality. In an instant, former child soldiers can come to believe that all the dangers of war still surround them, impinging on their daily routine of life. These haunting and nightmarish experiences return without warning and when least desired. They can be drawn to mind by subtle triggers: a smell, a specific song, or even the look on someone's face.

Flashbacks and nightmares are not just remembrances of the past. No, the child soldier is transported back to the moment of danger and reexperiences that event in the present moment. Unless there is intervention and healing, it is likely that a formerly abducted child soldier might never leave the war behind.

A few sessions with a mental health professional can have a huge positive impact on these youths and on how they see their future. In this region of Africa, the opportunities to receive such mental health care are very slim and in some areas, practically nonexistent. Some former child soldiers have never seen a mental health care professional, even though they have been forced to engage in countless brutal slayings, including killing people they love just to satisfy their rebel captors. The ratio of doctors to patients in this region of the world is 1 to 25,000. When it comes to mental health care, gaining access to a mental health care professional to get the help one needs to heal is even more reduced.

Beyond differences of skin color, language, culture, economic status, and distance from us, we are one human family. In essence, there is no such thing as other people's children. The youth who have endured violence and afflictions in African war zones are our children too. The fact that these children receive little or no mental health care after surviving the perils of war as child soldiers is inexcusable. It is at the same time a summons to us to reach out to them with the care that is desperately needed. In our linked and limited world, this task will demand creative and imaginative use of our resources dedicated to them and their well-being.

U.S. military personnel returning from the war zones in Iraq and Afghanistan are required to meet with a mental health specialist. In past generations, returning soldiers were given the option for such care. It is now compulsory, because it has become clearer than in previous generations that war exacts a heavy toll on the inner life of combatants—the emotional and spiritual self. It also exacts a heavy price on the families of all those who are left behind as their sons and daughters are sent to fight. Family life suffers from all the myriad ways that war intrudes into our hopes for the future.

Ought there not to be a massive, global recognition that former child soldiers, wherever they live, deserve the same mental health care we give our returning soldiers? Ought we to not be a part of that effort?

Attention to the Realm of the Spirit

The government of Uganda has primarily relied on a military strategy to end this conflict. Military aggression against the LRA, regardless of its merits as a political or military strategy, is tantamount to inflicting violence against children. Both the rebels and the Ugandan government have seemed indifferent to whether these children come out of the war alive or dead. Therefore these LRA youths, instead of learning to trust their elders to provide for their safety, have learned from them that they are disposable people. Their own government, as well as their rebel captors, reinforce this fear-provoking message by their actions. Fear, instead of trust, is what has been inculcated into their character for years.

With the militarization of northern Uganda, the children have gradually come to sense that their worth is principally derived from their ability to engage in battle and contribute to the war effort, not from who they are as persons. Gradually child soldiers can come to perceive all of life's relationships, even those that are most personal and intimate, through the narrow prism of utility.

The fact that child soldiers are introduced to exploitative relationships very early on in life has profound, far-reaching consequences.

Valued for what they do, not prized for who they are, they can naturally be expected to internalize the lesson that "you are what you do." That message is especially pernicious since what they are forced to do is harm and kill others. When they are removed from the war situation and have some distance between themselves and the danger they once knew, some former youths of the LRA are racked with shame when they remember the violence they did to others.

While the wounded bodies, distorted minds, and broken spirits of war-traumatized youth need careful, loving attention to heal, it is their spirits that deserve primary focus. It is clear to many who have spent sizeable amounts of time with formerly abducted child soldiers that their greatest deprivation lies in the realm of the spirit. They feel unworthy of love—God's love as well as ours. Their spirits are languishing in a predicament from which they see no possible escape. This has resulted chiefly from an utter breakdown of trusting relationships. There is little or no belief or trust in the power of goodness. They have lived for so long a time without such goodness they no longer believe in its power.

The virtue of trust is an overarching one in the spiritual life. We learn to trust while we are still young. We are encouraged to trust in the goodness of God, the goodness of our parents, and the goodness of the world surrounding us. This has not been at all the lived experience of the youth in the LRA. All bonds of trust have been systematically frayed and then broken for them. Instead, these youths have known humiliation in the extreme, loneliness, isolation, and a long privation of loving and trusting relationships. Under such conditions the spirit languishes.

It is a rare joy for me to see my friend Sunday Obote trust the adult world around him again. He suffered greatly when his family could no longer protect him from the rebels when they stormed his home and hauled him away. The beginnings of trust now emerging in his life after six years of freedom contain also the beginnings of life in the spirit. At age twenty-one, he asked to receive Eucharist for the first time, signaling to his catechists and adult mentors that while inner healing is happening slowly, he has not given up on life nor on God's hand lifting him up.

Forgiveness is a key component to the redemption of all persons. It is especially evident in the redemption of those who have killed. Until the youth of the LRA are guided on a path that first leads to their seeking forgiveness for the wrongs they committed, reconciliation and mercy will elude them. Just as these child soldiers were instructed by the rebels to do evil actions, now those truly interested and committed to their well-being must show them another path. It is not enough to simply condemn an action by another. Such action must also be countered by an opposite force for good.

Reconciliation and mercy are prized blessings that may occur at the end of a journey marked by honestly acknowledging one's own complicity in wrongdoing accompanied by sincere remorse for injuries caused. The child soldiers of the LRA are not strong enough in spirit to make that journey alone. They need spiritual counselors and companions to help and guide them to make the choices that lead to healing and new life.

Together with Archbishop Odama and a leading catechist of the region, John Bosco Komakech, I helped establish in 2002 the St. Kizito Scholarship Fund. One of the principal initiatives it has just completed is the construction of a large counseling center in the heart of the city of Gulu that has become a popular gathering place for many youths who are now freed from the LRA war. It is staffed by both trained catechists and counselors who give special attention to the needed inner healing of war-traumatized youth. Over five hundred young people are currently being served through this outreach program.

The story of the LRA child soldiers is still being written every day that these individuals long inwardly for a healing and an absolution of the evil they were engaged in while in the custody of the rebels. Some have still not even found a way to begin to forgive themselves and so are still trapped, imprisoned in a suffering that just will not go away.

A Summons to Solidarity

Imagine encountering a wounded, hurting child crying for help and that young person is looking directly at you. It is certain that you will interrupt whatever activities you were occupied with and immediately offer your help in comforting that child, eliminating whatever caused that child's hurt. Now imagine encountering hundreds upon hundreds

Former child soldiers in school

of wounded, hurting children all around you, crying for help, and you also sense they are looking in your direction. You can ask Jason Russell, Bobby Bailey, and Laren Poole what they did when they found themselves in precisely this position. They were budding filmmakers in their early twenties when they committed themselves to make the sacrifices entailed in an African sojourn in which they would document the unfolding genocide in the Darfur region of western Sudan.

An excursion of this magnitude necessitated their taking a considerable amount of time off from work and school. It meant risking the dangers that our African sisters and brothers face daily—chiefly, violence and disease. Laren became seriously ill with malaria, the number one killer in Africa. He was hospitalized for more than a month and needed a lengthy convalescence before being able to resume his work.

Before committing to the journey, they already sensed that there was a story unfolding in this region of the world that the rest of the world needed to hear and see. What they did not know is that the story they would eventually come to tell millions of Americans back home was happening not in Sudan but directly south, across the border in northern Uganda.

Our forebears just a century ago would find it outlandish to think that total strangers on the opposite side of the world could have such powerful effects on one another's lives as we clearly do today. We literally can be a saving presence in one another's lives. We can help contribute to one another exactly that which is missing for a whole, safe, and humanly worthwhile life.

These three young American filmmakers are not just altruistic idealists in pursuit of a utopian global peace. Rather, they are realistic young professionals who possess the conviction that their generation is hungering to make a difference in the lives of extremely vulnerable persons wherever they are found. They also hold to the belief that this pursuit will greatly enhance all of our lives.

Persons in North America who respond to injustice happening in the developing nations of Africa, Asia, Eastern Europe, and Latin America are coming to realize that it is also to our own benefit to be in solidarity with the most vulnerable and their aspirations for justice. As the world grows ever more interdependent, we are seeing how our own security is vitally connected to the security of the world's most impoverished and struggling peoples. Abject poverty and helplessness breed the kind of despair that fuels the engines of violent extremism all across the globe.

The painful stories of the child soldiers of Uganda will break your heart wide open if you allow them access to the deep places within your spirit. All the unseen and unknown children of our time who bear crushing burdens can be encountered in their eyes alone. If you listen with your heart to their voices you will be unable to turn away. All of humanity is propelled forward when we make a choice to be in solidarity with extremely vulnerable youth and help end the plight of children in armed conflict.

People in dire and dangerous situations, as are the children who walk nightly from their homes to sleep in safer environments because they fear rebel abductions, are encountered up close and personal through the medium of film, commanding our attention in riveting ways. This is what has happened in the making of the documentary film *Invisible Children*, which Russell, Bailey, and Poole created. It draws forth a strong and immediate emotional connection, while at the same time informing our minds and consciences about an intolerable situation in our world in which so many children are forced into armed conflict or have their entire lives disrupted by it.

Pope John XXIII, the jovial and often-smiling pope, taught us that when it comes to addressing the major social issues of our day a threefold approach of observe, judge, and act bears much merit.

It all begins with the power to observe one another, coming to know what joys and dangers our sisters and brothers face who live at a great distance from us. The power of film is unique in its ability to capture all those revealing images that shout out the truth for us.

The film *Invisible Children* captured the imagination of young people across the nation because the three artists who gave it to us had the grace and skill to document a currently unfolding drama in a way that draws us all in as characters. Their film gives us glimpses of ourselves. If a story about a small boy fighting to reclaim his humanity from rebel marauders does not make us think about our own struggles to be set free from our own demons, I doubt anything will move us. The film demands that we judge ourselves as we also must make judgments about the injustices that have rocked the youth of northern Uganda. In listening to the voices of the children in northern Uganda we can find our own best voice.

It is probably in the realm of rousing others into action that *Invisible Children* has had its paramount impact. It has spawned a whole movement of solidarity with war-torn northern Uganda. The children who have suffered for so long out of the gaze of the rest of the world are invisible no more. Political advocacy, consciousness-raising, and the creation and funding of income-generating activities that give sustenance to native northern Ugandans are all among *Invisible Children*'s direct outcomes.

As atrocities inflicted on the children of northern Uganda have come to light for North Americans in recent years, several serious questions strike us: Who is responsible for committing these grave offenses against innocent children? It would be easy to say that the rebels alone are to blame, but might not the responsibility extend further? Is the world community responsible for turning a blind eye to these events? Are individuals (you and I) at fault for not urgently sensing the call to solidarity arising within our consciences to stand with these vulnerable youth, who have no sure protection? Perhaps most controversially, in what sense are the child soldiers themselves innocent, and to what extent should they themselves be held responsible for the violence they inflicted on others?

These questions pose a moral dilemma for those who educate themselves about the plight of child soldiers. The fact that horrific harm has been done to an entire generation of Ugandan children living through this brutal conflict is indisputable. The same people, however, who agree that the situation is heart-wrenching will likely disagree regarding the distribution of responsibility. The moral ambiguity that confronts us when examining this conflict challenges our desire for easy answers and self-satisfied conclusions. As easy as it is to recognize the devastating consequences of this conflict, it is just as hard to understand its moral implications.

Perhaps our blindness to the needs of others near and far is caused, in part, by our incessant preoccupation with securing first our own comfort and security. This likely is what constrains many of us at times from taking the risk of reaching out in solidarity to extremely vulnerable persons who live at a great distance from us. Surprisingly, when we give of ourselves, who we are and what we possess, we are not left diminished but uplifted and enlivened. Our own health and humanity depend on our sharing ourselves generously with all others, excluding no one.

It is said that a picture is worth a thousand words. The images of these young people of Uganda must speak volumes, hopefully enough that their cry for solidarity will be heard around the world. Often in my youth, I was reminded that there were children starving in Africa, but this held little meaning for me other than the warning that I had better eat the meal before me. It was just a phrase meant to entice a child to action. Now, as I look at all I have before me and in my possession, I cannot help but see the faces of those I have spent time with in the war zone of Uganda. I am forever connected to them and now you are connected to them in a new way as you gain detailed knowledge of their plight and open your heart to their experience.

I share my stories so that my words can evoke solidarity, an outreach to these youths who question whether or not they have a future. Recently, I heard an updated version of the common phrase mentioned above: "If a picture is worth a thousand words, then an action is worth a thousand pictures." *Action* is what is needed in order to change the lives of the world's most vulnerable children. Prayer, compassion, financial support, labor, and so much more can help. Every moment of solidarity brings them one step closer to living a life fitting to God's most beloved.

In light of the lives these young people, our sons and daughters, have endured, the vision that the Christ Child Society has embraced for 115 years can serve as a simple, powerful reminder to us all: "Nothing is ever too much to do for a child."

Notes

1. To read the story of the abduction of the girls from St. Mary's, see Els De Temmerman, *Aboke Girls: Children Abducted in Northern Uganda* (Kampala: Fountain Publishers, 2001).

2. See Grace Akallo and Faith J. H. McDonnell, *Girl Soldier: A Story of Hope for Northern Uganda's Children* (Grand Rapids: Chosen Books, 2007).

3. Grace Akallo interview by Sheryl Henderson Blunt, as found in "The Devil's Yoke: A Young Woman Describes Her Former Life as a Slave of Rebel Soldiers," *Christianity Today*, December 21, 2007.

Epilogue
Is Peace Possible?

In northern Uganda, peace is not something familiar. For many years there has been nothing remotely like it, even in the imagination of the people. They dream of peace, of course, but they do not know what it looks like. The current conflict between the LRA and the Ugandan government of Yoweri Museveni has been a part of their lives for over twenty years. It has ebbed and flowed and then escalated to a level that displaced nearly everyone from their homes, destroyed the economy of Acholiland, and continues to attack the future of the young people who are drawn unwillingly into the war. Is there any hope of finding peace, of agreeing to end the struggle in northern Uganda?

Peace requires compromise and concession. Joseph Kony and the LRA have repeatedly stated their wishes for peace but they have attached their offers to unattainable conditions. And while President Museveni also claims that he wants peace, his actions often belie his words. The history of the war in northern Uganda is filled with attempts to discuss peace, but also with returns to violence.

The first significant attempt to establish peace was in late 1993 and early 1994. The talks were moving in a positive direction and seemed within hours of leading to an agreement before they abruptly ended. Hard-line attitudes and excessive demands by both sides contributed to the breakdown of the peace process.

In 1998, President Museveni firmly believed he would soon defeat the rebels, and thus felt no need for peaceful negotiations. Unfortunately, this military success did not happen and the brutal conflict continued. By late 2000, the LRA had moved its base of operation into southern Sudan and had some support from the Sudanese government. During the next few years, the LRA forces were much less active in northern Uganda.

In the early months of 2002, local leaders in northern Uganda tried to start peace talks with the LRA, with the permission of President Museveni. When Museveni's attempt to drive the LRA out of Sudan failed, Kony's rebels avoided capture and the LRA returned in strength to Uganda, equipped with new weapons and filled with anger at the failed military invasion. There was a significant increase in abductions and violence in 2002 and 2003 as the LRA resumed guerilla activities in Uganda in one of the most violent periods in the twenty-year conflict. Later that year the situation in northern Uganda became increasingly desperate, and the government began ordering the evacuation of villages, requiring residents to move to areas in or near camps set up for the displaced. It was during this time that the vulnerable children of northern Uganda became night commuters to avoid capture.

The first glimmer of hope came at the end of 2004, when an LRA spokesman broadcast a radio message to Uganda, announcing the rebel group's interest in working toward peace. Museveni's government agreed to a ceasefire, and on December 1, the LRA and Uganda held their first peace talks since 1994. At the close of the meeting, it was agreed that a permanent ceasefire would be signed on December 31. But this never happened.

The beginning of the most lasting effort to resolve the LRA-Museveni conflict was in June 2006. In a rare public interview, Joseph Kony expressed his desire for peace talks while denying his responsibility for the violence in northern Uganda. Each side made demands unacceptable to the other, including the government's demand that Kony surrender. Nonetheless, Museveni moved ahead, setting a deadline of July 31, 2006, for the surrender of LRA leaders.

Official negotiations began in Juba, Sudan, on July 14, 2006. Joseph Kony and his chief lieutenant, Vincent Otti, were not present, for fear of being arrested and turned over to the International Criminal Court at The Hague. Surprisingly, progress was made over the ten-day meeting, and the two groups were led by negotiators to reach an agreement to end the fighting. The Cessation of Hostilities agreement, signed on August 26, took effect three days later. The group agreed to a five-point agenda to be pursued in order to reach a permanent peaceful conclusion to this guerrilla war:

1. there would be a ceasefire and the LRA would assemble at a designated location;
2. both parties would tackle the root causes of the conflict;
3. both parties would agree on acceptable methods of accountability and reconciliation;
4. both parties would agree to terms for a permanent ceasefire;
5. both parties would agree to a process of demobilization, disarmament, and reintegration.

Over the succeeding months, many meetings were attempted, some with success and others resulting in anger and delay. The rebels made demands, the government made threats. Accusations of violating the ceasefire were leveled by both sides. Deadlines were set and missed. New versions of the ceasefire were drafted and signed repeatedly.

In April 2007, talks resumed in earnest and began to move forward productively. By the end of June, the second and third agenda items were agreed upon in principle, although further action was needed to gain input from the people of Uganda and an implementation plan was required.

In autumn 2007, first the Ugandan government negotiators and then the LRA team met with victims of the many atrocities throughout northern Uganda. The government focused first on satisfying the victims' needs for justice, and the LRA team centered its visits on apologizing to those who had been hurt by the enduring conflict.

In December, President Museveni officially announced that January 31, 2008, would be the deadline for concluding peace negotiations. He threatened military action at that time if the five agenda points were not agreed upon. Joseph Kony reacted angrily to this barely veiled threat, but maintained his commitment to continue the negotiation process. Scheduled meeting dates came and went without any progress.

As 2008 began, the talks were at a crucial point and negotiations were set to complete the third of the five agenda points. But Museveni's patience was wearing thin. He held strongly to his imposed deadline of January 31 to complete all negotiations. Threats of military action against Kony were made once more, as the president promised to capture the LRA leader and thus end the conflict. The LRA countered that the deadline was not feasible. It appeared as if the talks would end once again without reaching the goal.

As the deadline neared, attention was drawn away from the peace process and toward the political upheaval in Kenya. The firm commitment to a January 31 deadline wavered. And then, unexpectedly, Joseph Kony relieved his team of peace negotiators, appointing new ones only days before new talks were to begin. Contrary to all fears, January 31 was marked with a negotiation session and a new ceasefire agreement. The United States and the European Union joined in the talks and a new, aggressive deadline for ending the war was set for the end of February.

The process continues. Hope remains, since violence has not returned, but the end is not yet in sight. The popular puzzle called the Rubik's Cube comes to mind. It involves complex manipulations to line up blocks of color in the proper pattern. While it is possible to succeed at this game, it requires great skill. Even so, the puzzle can be solved. This is not so sure a thing with peace in Uganda.

Why is it so difficult for the two sides to come to a peaceful agreement when both claim to desire it? The reason involves a combination of cultural differences, mistrust, greed, inhumanity, deceit, unwillingness to compromise, stubbornness, and perhaps more. Perhaps the current situation will continue to improve. Perhaps the peace talks will finally be successful. There have been many positive signs and developments that encourage hope. Displaced people are slowly beginning to return to their homes, and members of the LRA claim to be committed to a resolution of the conflict. The question that remains is whether the two leaders, Joseph Kony and President Museveni, are truly committed to peace. Although Museveni is the leader of the country, he was once in the place Joseph Kony holds today. He rules because he forcibly took control in 1986.

What always remains at the center of this country's situation is the children. It is impossible to account for the many young lives that have been changed or destroyed since the first attempt at peace failed in 1994. The failure to work out differences has been so much more costly and means so much more than just extended conflict. The inability of adults to be able to settle differences, talk reasonably, and compromise has resulted in the most pain being inflicted on children and on families and on those who have no ability to make a difference, those least in control of their destinies. This is perhaps the greatest sin that has been committed. And the international community has been reticent to get involved.

Mere children, youth, young adults have suffered enormously under the guns and machetes of the LRA and the autocratic government of President Yoweri Museveni. For them the tactics of both the LRA and the Ugandan government have been like fire that has produced ashes. An Acholi proverb comes to mind: *Mac onywalo buru*— fire has begotten ashes. This proverb is sometimes an expression of regret, but often is used to encourage the young to use their energy wisely and completely. Today's Acholi children have been tested by fire—refined by a horrendous tragedy orchestrated by the LRA and tolerated, if not encouraged, by Museveni, whose soldiers at times have also mistreated the children of Acholiland.

Through this ordeal of fire, the children have come to see violence targeted at one's very own brothers and sisters as insanity. Like no other generation before them, they have internalized the tragedy of exploitative ideology and they are also in the process of purging themselves of its essential loneliness and lack of compassion. As they enter adulthood, and become responsible for the future of their land, they bring a renewed sense of commonweal, where no one is given or assumes power in order to exclude others from the many gifts that God gives to all, freely.

There is no going back. Uganda can, and hopefully will, move forward in peace. But the mark that has been left is indelible. Children have been forced to grow up way too soon, families have been broken, livelihoods have been destroyed. No one can know God's will. But the God of peace and justice that we believe in certainly would not choose such a devastating life for the youngest and the most vulnerable. Jesus taught us that God wishes peace for all people. God holds a preeminent place for the dignity of all human persons, but especially for the children. The young of northern Uganda, like all children everywhere, deserve to live lives filled with hope—hope for the future and, even more important, hope for the joy of living each day filled with love.

Acts of Solidarity with Child Soldiers
Observe, Judge, Act

On these pages, the reality of life as a child soldier, life in the relentless violence and poverty of war, has come alive. Uganda is but one example of many countries where the dignity of young human persons is destroyed. We must keep in mind always that God created us, every one of us, in his image and likeness and has endowed us with the right to life and love. With these rights comes a duty to act in a way that preserves the rights of all, especially the children.

The following are acts of solidarity, ways we can become more deeply immersed in the plight of those less fortunate, helping to bring human dignity to all God's children. In the words of filmmaker Gerard Straub, "Every act of mercy and kindness brings us closer to the reality of God."

Observe and Judge

1. The ministry of the San Damiano Foundation and its president, Gerard Straub, is dedicated to putting the power of film at the service of the poor. It has produced a moving documentary film depicting the difficult life in northern Uganda. In this film, you can meet Sunday Obote and many others whose lives have been deeply affected by the rebellion in Acholiland. If you can do only one small act, see this film. *The Fragrant Spirit of Life* will open your eyes to a very different world and will change your heart forever. The film can be purchased through the San Damiano Foundation, P.O. Box 1794, Burbank, CA 91507, www.sandamianofoundation.org.

2. Two other compelling films chronicle the struggles and the healing process that are ongoing in Uganda.

- The Evangelical Lutheran Church in America film *Uganda: Ready to Forgive, an African Story of Grace,* shows the power of forgiveness that is so strong in the Acholi culture, which has been so hurt by war. This film can be purchased at www.ecla .org. The film, hosted by Rwandan genocide survivor Immaculee Ilibagiza, brings to life God's mercy in humanity at its best.
- *Invisible Children* is a film produced by a group of young filmmakers in search of an adventure. The situation they found in northern Uganda changed their lives and led to the formation of a nonprofit organization of the same name, Invisible Children. This moving film can be purchased at www.invisible children.com. The Web site also has a list of showings throughout the country and an informative "Get Involved" page that is well worth a visit.

3. Ishmael Beah is a young man who lived the life of a child soldier in Sierra Leone in that country's civil war of the 1990s. The story of Ishmael Baeh is a profound story of courage and struggle. He tells his compelling story of his life on the run in *A Long Way Gone.* This book, published by Farrar, Straus, and Giroux, can be purchased at most bookstores.

Act

The St. Kizito Scholarship Fund (now St. Kizito Foundation) was founded in 2001 by Father Donald Dunson as a way to help bring the children in Africa out of poverty and harm's way and into the secure pleasures of childhood. One hundred percent of the monies raised are used to pay for the many needs of the children. You have already contributed to the St. Kizito Project by purchasing this book, as all of the author's royalties are donated to the children. Donations of every size can be helpful. As children in the United States shop in preparation for the new school year, consider providing for the schooling of the children of St. Kizito as well. Also consider making this part of your annual school shopping. Donations can be sent to St. Kizito Foundation, 28700 Euclid Ave., Wickliffe, Ohio 44092.

Red Hand Day is celebrated on February 12. On February 12, 2002, the *Optional Protocol to the Convention on the Rights of the Child on the Involvement of Children in Armed Conflict* entered into force with ninety-two different nations as signatories. This agreement was aimed at stopping the use of child soldiers throughout the world. Celebrate Red Hand Day each year by praying for the end to the practice of using the young as soldiers, by spreading the word—informing a friend, relative, or co-worker about the plight of the child soldiers, or by finding a place to join in Red Hand Day activities. More information is available at www.redhandday.org.

The only way to permanently change the lives of the child soldiers is peace. Make prayer for peace throughout the world your priority. Choose a special time each day, or each week, and spend five minutes in prayer. A peace prayer written by Pope John Paul II is included at the end of this book. It is a wonderful way to give prayerful support to our brothers and sisters in need.

The cost of a jerry can for carrying water from wells to homes is approximately US$2. Feeding a family of four for a week in Uganda costs approximately $10. Make a commitment to a small sacrifice each week or month in your home. As a family, share a small, simple meal together and earmark the savings for the plight of these children who are part of our worldly family. Research and decide together where your donation should be sent.

Gerard Thomas Straub

Uganda's future

Prayer for Peace

To you,
>
> Creator of nature and humanity,
> of truth and beauty,
> I pray.

Hear my voice,
>
> for it is the voice of victims of all wars and violence
> among individuals and nations.

Hear my voice,
>
> for it is the voice of all children who suffer
> and will suffer
> when people put their faith in weapons and war.

Hear my voice,
>
> when I beg you to instill
> into the hearts of all human beings
> the wisdom of peace, the strength of justice,
> and the joy of fellowship.

Hear my voice,
>
> for I speak for the multitudes in every country
> and every period of history
> who do not want war
> and are ready to walk the road of peace.

Hear my voice,
>
> and grant insight and strength
> so that we may always respond
> to hatred with love,
> to injustice with total dedication to justice,
> to need with sharing of self,
> to war with peace.

O God, hear my voice,
>
> and grant into the world
> Your everlasting peace. Amen.

—Pope John Paul II
"Hear My Voice," Hiroshima Peace Memorial
February 25, 1981
© Libreria Editrice Vaticana
Used with permission